HOMO SAPIENS

A SPECIES GONE APE

Mark Gerszewski

Cover Design

A special thanks to artist extraordinaire Sarah Kobezak of Williamsburg, Virginia, for her artwork and cover design. Please visit her studio website at www.kobezakartworks.com.

Website/Blog

Keep up with Mark Gerszewski's latest literary projects by visiting www.markgerszewski.com.

Charities

Ten percent of the profits from this book will go to two different charities that are close to my heart: Eight percent will go to my first charity, the Wounded Warrior Project. Please visit their website at www.woundedwarriorproject.org. Remember, the greatest casualty is being forgotten! Two percent will go to my second charity, the Marie Gerszewski Nursing Scholarship Endowment Fund at Norfolk State University, Norfolk, Virginia; because no nurse should ever be half trained on how to insert a catheter. Please visit their website at www.nsu.edu.

Special Thanks

Books are never complete without an inner circle of friends who, at times, you wouldn't give a second thought to choking the living crap out of.

In no particular order, I would like to sincerely thank Don Hammer for his feedback, his editing work, and his comments, particularly in the areas of adolescent upbringing. I would like to thank Morgan Tibar for her research and cross-checking; Leslie Metzger, Jesse Collins, John Hoffman, and Lauren Blank for a variety of support and feedback along the way; Roger Knowles, Rob Morris, and Ahmed Tibar for their technological advice and help in putting together my website and pitch videos; and Greg Page for unofficially being my official photographer. Last, but certainly not least, I would like to thank Ann Westerman for her early support, guidance, inspiration, and encouragement in my writing endeavors. She is probably the only one I *don't* want to choke the living crap out of.

To *all* of you, I profess a deep and appreciative thank you!

Contents

Contents

Introduction

When I was a child and throughout my adolescence, my parents said things that still resonate with me as powerfully as they ever have or ever will. They weren't things that were repeated with such redundancy that I could not help but remember them, such as, "Get your elbows off the table" or "Sit up straight" while eating at the dinner table. (Once upon a time, families would actually sit down together to a home-cooked meal at the dining room table, turn off the television, and converse about their day. And guess what? It wasn't Thanksgiving; it was Tuesday.) No, those things were said infrequently and without luster, yet repeated often enough over fifteen or twenty years that they permeated my brain.

I never knew my great-grandfather, a German immigrant who, in 1872, stepped off a steamer onto a plot of dry land known as Battery Park. (It would be another twenty years before Ellis Island would become the immigrant inspection station for immigrants arriving from Europe.) He headed west, as many of them did in those days, settled in Dakota Territory, fought Indians, built a sod-roofed log cabin, raised a family, and lived off the land. He was hardworking, God-fearing, and uneducated (or at least uneducated in the "formal education" sense of the word). But then again, I don't know many "formally educated" folk, even by 1800s standards, to whom you could hand a knife, a week's provisions, a horse, and the clothes on their back and say, "Here. Go out in the middle of this God-forsaken wilderness and make a life for yourself and your family." And yet he did.

My mother would quote my great-grandfather, saying, "Educated people are some of the dumbest people I know." As a child, those words went in one ear and out the other, but as the years passed, I began to realize that perhaps, and even with certainty, my great-grandfather knew something that educated people didn't.

Mark Twain once said, "When I was a boy of fourteen, my father was so ignorant I could hardly stand to have the old man around. But when I got to be twenty-one, I was astonished at how much the old man had learned in seven years."[1] My father, too, was an astonishing learner. He was also hardworking, God-fearing, and uneducated.

In 1933, my father dropped out of high school and joined the Civilian Conservation Corps to help support his parents and siblings during the Great Depression. In the spring of 1940, he was fortunate enough to be accepted into the US Navy. A year and a half later, he survived the Japanese attack on Pearl Harbor and spent the next six months recovering from his injuries in a naval hospital. That was his formal education.

"Human beings are the dumbest species on the face of the earth," my "ignorant" father used to say. He would continue rambling on and on about animals and how they have no formal education, yet they develop the most acute instincts; how birds migrate thousands of miles every year with the changing of the seasons and find themselves back in the exact same place without the benefit of maps or road signs (we didn't have GPS back then). Or how salmon, born in freshwater streams, make their way downstream into the salty Pacific where they live and travel thousands of miles; then one day, with fierceness and tenacity, they fight their way back upstream to the place of their birth, spawn, and die. My father was intrigued by those sensational acts of Mother Nature and by the fact that, in contrast, human beings seemed to be losing any and all rationale that should be innate in all of us—common sense. "Even an amoeba, a brainless, single-cell organism, has the intelligence to shy away from danger in its environment," my father would continue to blab. But as Mark Twain so eloquently pointed out, by the time I was twenty-one, I began to realize that perhaps, and even with certainty, he knew something that I didn't.

How far have we as a species evolved from the not-too-distant past of our more recent forefathers? What did our grandfathers and great-grandfathers try to teach us that we can't seem to comprehend? Why is it that with all the modern-day conveniences we have to make our lives more comfortable—conveniences that our great-grandfathers could only dream of, if they could even imagine them at all—we as a society are as depressed and unhappy as ever? Why can't we seem to learn from history that has repeated itself since the beginning of civilization? Do we really think we are that special or that immune from repeating historical mistakes once again? Don't answer that…it was rhetorical.

Homo Sapiens: A Species Gone Ape is a study of our modern-day human nature, how we got here, and where we are going socially, culturally, and economically.

Many of the discussions and examples expressed in this book may seem to be exclusive to the United States. This is only because the author is American and lives in America, so most of his experiences are specific to the United States. However, I can assure you that Homo sapiens inhabit the entire earth and that many, if not all, of the cultural dilemmas discussed in this book, in one form or another, are a concern of our entire species, not one's specific nationality.

Section 1:

The Birthing Canal

In The Beginning...
There Was Reason

In the beginning there was reason,
and there was a reason for it.
But then on the sixth day, God created
man...and everything went to hell.

If you believe in the Bible's version of creation, then you could arguably say that day six was the turning point in the brief history of the world, when things started to go south. Or, if you're a Darwinist, then you could arguably cite countless historical references as to when the world as we know it (either in today's terms or from a historical perspective) began to go south. I suppose the reason for this ambiguity in pointing to a specific evolutionary turning point lies in the fact that there have been so many instances or periods of devastating social, cultural, and economic decline in civilization that it's hard to definitively point the finger at who started this cycle we humans seem to enjoy so much. Like the sequel of a sequel of what was once a decent movie now turned bad, we just can't seem to get enough of it!

Every societal cataclysmic event or period that man has ever experienced has either been environmental in nature (Mount Vesuvius) or man-made (building Pompeii right next to Mount

Vesuvius). Except for a meteor the size of New York City hitting the earth, the Ice Age rolling around again, or an all-out Martian attack, all of the world's "dark ages" have been man-made. After all, Vesuvius didn't kill Pompeii. Building Pompeii right next to Vesuvius killed Pompeii. Today Mount Vesuvius is still active, still one of the most dangerous volcanos in the world, and still inhabited by approximately one million people who live in dangerously close proximity to it. The next time the volcano throws a tantrum, the world will be stunned at the devastation (actually more like dumbfounded). We will sit in our comfortable living rooms, staring at our fifty-two inch flat screen TVs, watching CNN in shock and horror as a good many of these one million or so inhabitants will be crying the blues because their homeowner's insurance policy doesn't cover the wrath of Vesuvius. And even though they have known the potential danger ever since they bought their house, they will still point the finger at the town, and even Italy herself, for compensation that is rightly theirs for allowing them to live so close to this disaster waiting to happen.

Today's worldly worries and the decline of our species are in stark comparison to the ruin of Pompeii, and more specifically, the fall of the Roman Empire. I am not the first to make this comparison, nor will I be the last. The fact that more and more people (even "formally educated" people—yikes!) are making this analogy should tell us something, at least get us to stop and think, or perhaps make us stop, ponder, and ask some sobering questions. But *no*, not us!

Many historians disagree on the specific culprit that perpetuated the fall of the Roman empire, but most agree that it was a multitude of reasons, not one defining factor: the fragmenting of the family unit, the decay of morality, the decline of the Roman population, upper-echelon prosperity that came with the conquest of foreign lands and peoples, a failing economy and unemployment of the working class, political corruption, invasions from foreign enemies, allowing Germanic mercenaries to infiltrate the ranks of the Roman military, civil fighting within the Roman military, and a weakened central government. It makes you wonder: Are we talking about the year 300 or 2013?

I'm sure many will disagree on a specific culprit perpetuating today's decline of the human race. I'm sure some will even argue that there's no decline at all. At the risk of getting the intellectual gears turning, allow me to be so bold as to propose a few possibilities of my own.

The unsurpassed economic prosperity that began following the Second World War, and continued for approximately sixty years into the dawn of the twenty-first century, could very well be the catalyst that got the proverbial ball rolling. Now don't get me wrong: I'm not blaming capitalism, as many are, and I certainly believe in a free market society, but I also believe in the great yin-yang. There is always some negative impact to anything good and vice versa. (If that's too "Eastern" for you, we can simply refer to it as the "unintended consequences" of our actions.) Sometimes that unintended consequence takes years to emerge, but sooner or later, it rears its ugly head. Economic prosperity, especially being born into it as the last several generations have, has made us lazy, complacent, and lethargic. I'm not suggesting that all people in today's developed world are lazy and unmotivated, but we most certainly lack the ambition of our forefathers who lived in the first half of the twentieth century. Much of their hard work and ambition, in a time when many did not have electricity, indoor plumbing, or even an automobile (not to mention satellite TV and a remote to boot), was out of a necessity to provide for the basic needs of their families, and they toiled laboriously to do so. Most, if not all, of the people that I have had the privilege of knowing from my father's generation, those who lived through the Great Depression of the

1930s, lived their whole lives with a disciplined respect for money. They lived comfortably but modestly in their retirement years, always with a conscientious sense of inheritance for their children. That discipline is in distinct contrast to today's generation that, in general, lives well beyond its financial means, then bitches and complains because making ends meet is a struggle. This ideology has morphed into other disastrous economic conditions, namely a state of dependence. This is an entitlement mentality where, instead of working to correct our own individual financial improprieties, we look to other entities with our hands outstretched to replenish the coffers. This presumably worked just swell for the past forty years or so, but now, with most of the industrialized world in serious economic distress and on the verge of global financial collapse, we don't seem to care as long as we keep getting our piece of the rhubarb pie, perpetuating the inevitable. Didn't JFK say, "Ask not what your country can do for you; ask what you can do for your country"?[1] Or was I just dreaming?

Once prosperity began to take hold, we then added the social revolution of the '60s to the mix, fanning the flames of our frenzy. Instead of reinventing the wheel on this one, I would like to defer to Joe Queenan's book, *Balsamic Dreams: A Short But Self-Important History of the Baby Boomer Generation*. In this book, Joe so eloquently and poignantly (and humorously, I might add) points out that baby boomers were the first generation in American history to be born directly into the lap of luxury. They had it all—the money, the attitude, and the freedom to make a difference. They were "rebels with a cause," out to change the world. But in the end, they sold their dreams and their visions and the only thing they really became good at was making money. In the process, they became the most pretentious and obnoxious generation ever, whose idealistic dreams of changing the world faded into a cultural ideology that favored lifestyle over life and pop culture over culture. I don't mean to paraphrase Joe's book, but I strongly suggest that, if you want a good laugh and an eye opener, you should read it.

The collateral damage caused by these wannabe rebels has had far-reaching effects on society. Take feminism for instance—it's just one example of many that will be explored in gory detail in the pages to come. The woman's rights and woman's suffrage movements that sprang up in the nineteenth and twentieth centuries were just and worthy causes that brought to light many inequalities in our society. Throw the wannabe rebels of the '60s into the mix, forget to stir the pot, and presto, what do you get? You get what's stuck to the bottom: feminism. You get partial-birth abortion, feticide (there's a word we haven't heard much since the days of the Roman empire), unsupervised kids, nannies (*au pair*, excuse me!), fragmenting of the family unit, no father figures or immediate role models, affirmative action (anyone who has ever lost a job to a lesser-qualified individual knows all about this one), quotas, and the list goes on!

And now that many of you feminists out there have your panties all in a bunch, I would like to remind you that there are many within your own ranks who agree you have gone too far. Your just and worthy rebellion of the '60s has given you an unimpeded license to go where no man has gone before.

Susan B. Anthony: I'm sorry, darling, but you'd better roll over and tell Harriet Tubman the news!

Sometime in the mid-seventies, my parents purchased our first microwave after several years of resisting the urge. My father often cited that we didn't need one, that the stove was much better. But I think he was just worried about getting cancer. Our first color television was purchased from Sears a couple of years earlier. The remote control for the TV was a device called "son," as in "Son, get up and change the TV to channel 13. Lawrence Welk is on in five minutes" or "Son, what is this crap you're watching? Get up and change the channel." (Something that I'm sure would be looked upon in today's society as child abuse.) The same "remote" was used to open and close the garage door and also served as an answering machine to take messages for our home-based rotary-style phone—a lovely peachy, flesh-tone colored phone with matching slinky cord that firmly grounded us to the operator, Myrtle, who was miles away, chain-smoking at her refrigerator-sized switchboard, connecting, disconnecting, and redirecting calls all day long with a vengeance. Life was good! But then one day, this guy named Bill Gates came along, dropped out of college, invented interfacing operating software in his garage, and screwed up the world forever.

Yes, the advent of the home computer and electronic age was upon us, and so was the beginning of the end. All the ingredients needed for the dumbing down of our species were in place, and no one was stirring the pot. The next round of monumental mankind stupidity was clearly taking shape, and, over the next three decades, human beings would become "the biggest loser" in the most popular and realistic reality TV show ever, titled *How Pathetic Are We?*

"I'll take Idiocracy for eight hundred, Alex."

"Idiocracy for eight hundred, and ohhh, it's the Daily Double, Tom. How much would you like to wager?"

"Uhhh, everything, Alex."

"Now, Tom, you do realize that you're already at negative sixteen hundred. If you get it right, you'll still be in last place at zero, and if you get it wrong, you'll be at negative thirty-two hundred, just like a Bernie Madoff Ponzi scheme."

"I'm willing to take that risk, Alex."

"Yes, aren't we all, Tom? OK, for sixteen hundred dollars, here we go! The answer is— blue."

The audience waits with bated breath as the lovely *Jeopardy* (*How Pathetic Are We?*) music plays: Do – Do – Do – Do – Do – Do – Do – Doot – Dadoot – Da – Do – Do – Do!

"Time is up. Do you have the answer, Tom?"

"Yes. What is the color of your eyes, Alex?"

"Oh no, I'm sorry, Tom. The correct answer is, 'What was Kurt Cobain immediately before and after he blew his head off?' Join us tomorrow, ladies and gentlemen, for another exciting edition of *How Pathetic Are We?* Tomorrow's contestants will be the all-star casts from *The Kardashians*, *Teen Mom*, and *Bridezillas*, all out to prove that no adult is smarter than an invertebrate! I'm Alex Trebek. Good night!"

Yes, the dawn of the electronic age was the turning point where the '60s revolutionaries began to cash in their dreams of change for cold hard cash. Once again, don't get me wrong. I'm not blaming Mr. Gates, Mr. Allen, Mr. Jobs, Mr. Wozniak, or any other college dropout, garage working, forerunning entrepreneur of the computer age for our societal metamorphosis into the abyss. After all, technology and change aren't inherently bad; in fact, change is inevitable. The crime is how we, Homo sapiens, take for granted, abuse, and then justify our abuse of these *gifts* of our own making.

Our forefathers who were young adults during the great depression of the 1930s and who lived long enough to see the side effects of the '60s Cultural Revolution, innately knew something was amiss. They understood that a generation with that much money, power, and freedom without an appreciation or historical perspective of where it came from was destined to repeat history on a scale the human race had never seen before.

And so, without further ado, let us examine a few of the modern-day cultural and humanistic errors of our ways.

And on the seventh day God rested.
And He's been stressed ever since.

Teach Your Children Well

---

*T*his past Christmas holiday, I was at a friend's house trying to drown my dismay and disdain for the human race while celebrating and honoring the arrival of baby Jesus. I was making every effort to enjoy myself, and I must say that my Sailor Jerry and Coke on the rocks was most instrumental in stimulating my Christmas spirit. The home was beautifully decorated. The Christmas tree was picture perfect—right out of the special holiday edition of *Good Housekeeping*—standing tall and bright, emanating the sweet pine scent of the season. The soft, endearing sounds of Michael Bublé singing "I'll Be Home for Christmas" permeated the air. I would have preferred a Marlene Dietrich version or good old Bing or even Harry Connick Jr., but this is to be expected from a young, modern yuppie family, and I wasn't about to let something so mundane dampen my alcohol-induced spirits. The memorable aroma of the impending four-course meal kept us eating hors d'oeuvres in moderation the best we could. The stockings were hung with great care below the Christmas cards with accompanying family photographs, which were neatly arranged on the fireplace mantle in the same fashion as the individuals in the photos themselves. The gas logs in the fireplace burned so eloquently that if it were not for the absence of the occasional *crack* or *pop*, I would have sworn it was a genuine, old-fashioned, honest-to-goodness fire with real logs purchased from Sam's Club that were made in China with child labor working in deforestation camps, every one of whom were endearingly grateful to their omnipotent supreme leader for the privilege of their substandard wage and substandard working condition job. Where is Norman Rockwell when you need him?

When the dinner feast was over, we retired to the living room with our sherry and our cognac to relax, converse, and enjoy each other's company. The children, who were not nestled all safe in their beds, began to show signs of fatigue from a busy and napless day playing with their cousins. Three rug rats between the ages of four and six were starting to get out of hand, and so it was that one of the fathers finally put his foot down, stepped in, and said enough is enough.

"Gertrude!" the stern disciplinarian said. (The names have been changed to protect the guilty from ever being properly disciplined.) Gertrude did not respond. "Gertrude!" the voice of reason spoke again. Gertrude obviously thought that the calling of her name two times meant that she must immediately flee the area since she sped out of the room and into the back family room, accompanied by her two screaming friends. The relaxing of the adults continued. A few minutes later, Gertrude was back running, laughing, and screaming through the living room with her entourage in tow.

"Gertrude, stop running!" the evil fascist dictator demanded. "Gertrude, come here!" The little ones passed through one door, out the other, and they were gone again.

"They're so cute," Mussolini stated.

"They're having so much fun," Mrs. Mussolini replied.

Over the next fifteen minutes or so, the children's behavior became so distracting that I was no longer able to enjoy myself,

regardless of how much spiced rum and Coke I drank. The behavior was compounded tenfold by the constant annoyance of the
inept dictators constantly barking, "Gertrude this" and "Gertrude
that." I succumbed to the fact that the rest of the evening was
going to be a living hell, so I decided to conduct a little experiment. For the next hour, I counted how many times Mussolini and
his wife spoke Gertrude's name in an authoritative tone. Forty-
three times in sixty minutes was the final tally. After I finished my
mathematical computations, I faked a yawn, politely thanked my
fascist hosts, retrieved my coat, and called it a night. Now there's a
Norman Rockwell for the ages.

What amazed me, aside from the fact that the parents were
totally ineffective and worthless when it came to providing any
form of discipline for their children, was the fact that the parents
seemed to be oblivious as to how annoying, distracting, and inconsiderate it was for their children to behave that way in front
of guests during such a festive event. It was as if it was completely
normal and acceptable behavior. (Of course, it was normal behavior and certainly acceptable by the masses of others on the same
side, and only misunderstood by us outsiders who couldn't possibly understand it in the first place.) Back in my day, we were
spanked, got our mouths washed out with soap, we were sent to
our rooms, went without dinner, or all of the above for being half
as inconsiderate as the youth of today. But then again, we weren't
as privileged, were we?

Several months ago, I was speaking to a woman I know who
runs a child day care. I don't remember what we were talking
about, but the subject of discipline came up. I was surprised to
hear that you can't even put kids in "time-out" anymore because it
is considered isolation, and children can't be isolated as a form of
punishment. The correct response of the day (or should I say, the
moment?) is to put them in their "quiet corner" or their "thinking

chair" so that they are still with the group, not isolated, yet not overstimulated either. For hundreds and hundreds of years, perhaps even thousands of years, children were pretty much disciplined in the same fashion: with a good ol' spanking when they needed it. The baby boomers came along and suddenly, they had a better way. Twenty years later, that's no good anymore. Here's an even better way. Twenty years from now, there will be yet another socially acceptable way. How do all you evil parents feel now that you have been putting your kids in "time-out" for the past fifteen to twenty years and come to find out you have been isolating them, no doubt leading to long-term psychotherapy? Then we sit around and wonder, analyze, discuss, engage in serious debate, and conduct study after study (many of which are paid for by you and me—Mr. & Mrs. Taxpayer) about why a record number of adults today are on Prozac and a whole buffet of other antidepressants. Is it possible that during their entire fragile, impressionable developing years, they have been sheltered from anything and everything bad, offensive, disruptive to the pristine bubble they live in, or, God forbid, something that is insulting or could hurt their precious feelings? Do parents today know the meaning of "tough love"? As a parent of two children myself, I now know what my parents meant when they said, "It's going to hurt me more than it's going to hurt you," when enforcing "tough love" discipline—a statement that many parents of today know nothing about, and today's children will never know. Don't even get me started on the whole "1, 2, 3" technique for getting children to conform; or should I say the "1, 2, 2¼, 2½, 2¾, 3" technique? Nine out of ten times I have seen it used it hasn't worked. The kids understand that it doesn't work, but apparently the parents haven't got a clue. If any of you "1, 2, 3" disciplinarians out there are listening, it doesn't work because, in the end, you never enforce it anyway, and secondly, I'm sorry to inform you, but your prodigious four-year-old doesn't yet comprehend the concept of fractions.

Some time ago, a friend of mine told me a story that gets under my skin even to this day. He has a daughter who is one of these quintessential modern-day parents who don't believe in spanking their kids. One evening, the daughter, son-in-law, and twenty-month-old grandson were over for dinner. The grandson was misbehaving, playing with his food, and not responding to his mother's constant and incessant pleas to stop. Having had about as much as he could handle, my friend reached over and smacked his grandson on the wrist. Never having been swatted before, the grandson screamed bloody murder, the daughter jumped angrily to rescue her son from the clutches of evil, while the spineless father sat in quiet protest, only to spew venom about his father-in-law in the safe confines of his car on the way home (I'm sure). Today the grandson, who is four, behaves quite maturely around his grandfather, and if he does begin to get out of line, it only takes one verbal prompting by his grandfather to get him to behave. The parents, however, continue to have behavioral issues with him. OK, here's where the story really pisses me off. Whenever the grandson misbehaves around his parents, in an effort to get him to behave, they tell him that they're going to call granddad if he continues. Sweetie, if you don't have the backbone to discipline your kids with a swat on the behind when they need it, then you don't get to use your father as a scapegoat for discipline.

Does being a good, caring, and compassionate parent mean that kids should get away with murder? That no discipline is good discipline? That kids can't even learn the meaning of the word "no"? And we sit around, scratch our heads, and wonder why our teenage son or daughter doesn't listen to us or show us the slightest hint of respect. Or worse yet, our kid just shot three of his high school classmates because he was being bullied and couldn't deal with it!

The seeds of any civilization are rooted in our children, for they are the future of our species. And when the roots of a sapling are not nurtured properly they grow weak and the slightest gust of wind will topple the sapling never to rise again.

Anne Sullivan, thanks to their loving, misguided, parents, we now have a whole society of deaf, dumb, and blind kids that desperately need your attention. The bright side? They sure can play pinball!

The Agony of Defeat

B ack in the '70s, there was a sports TV show called *Wide World of Sports*. It had a great slogan—"The thrill of victory, and the agony of defeat." I can still picture that guy losing it as he came down the ski jump when they said "the agony of defeat." I guess you had to be there.

Kids begin learning competitive sports at a young age. Usually around five or six years old, parents will sign them up for their first team sport, typically soccer, basketball, T-ball, or flag football. It's a great concept, but a bad idea for the modern-day family. It's a bad idea because the whole concept of why the child is there to begin with is oftentimes distorted, misconstrued, and turned into a social experiment for the parents instead of being a fun learning experience for the child. It's kind of like the sick, demented reality show *Toddlers & Tiaras*.

On one hand, we don't want our little ones to be disappointed. We don't want them to feel like losers. Some parents don't even want to keep score, and, win or lose, everyone gets a trophy when it's all said and done. Instead of giving the child a high five and saying, "Well, son, you lost. How about we go home and work on those batting skills in the backyard?" we smother the child in BS by saying, "You were so good," "I'm so proud of you," "You did your best, and that's all that counts." Unfortunately, in the real world, it doesn't matter if you tried your best; it's the results you get that count. It's the bottom line that's important. Try telling your boss that it's OK that your department lost money in the last quarter, and that the loss is irrelevant because you and your team of coworkers tried your best to make money, and that you, Mr. Boss, are being overly critical and insensitive to the situation. Yeah, I can't wait to watch that one on YouTube.

As if that behavior isn't counterproductive enough, then we jump up and down, scream and pitch a fit because the neighborhood dad who volunteered his time to help coach your pain-in-the-ass ADD, ADHD son when he could be home watching *Mob Wives*, just made a questionable call! Let me explain something, kids playing competitive sports (and there is a reason why they call it "competitive" sports) just want to have fun! They just want to go out, get out of the house for a while, interact with other kids, and kick, or hit, or throw the ball around. The jury is still out on whether or not little Johnny is going to be the next Michael Jordan, so just relax and let the little one have some fun every once in a while. In the process, hopefully he will develop some basic motor skills and learn a little bit about the game, sportsmanship, and losing. If he begins showing a passion for the sport, and begins working at it five days a week on his own accord without prompting, then you as the parent can decide how much support you're going to give him in his first big endeavor in life. If he continues to excel in the activity, makes the high school varsity team as a freshman, gets a fully paid scholarship to a first-rate university, gets picked up by the big boys in a first-round draft pick, and is lucky enough to avoid serious injury in the process, then you, Mom and Dad, may sit on the sidelines and scream at Mr. Four-Eyes, Blind-as-a-Bat referee. In the meantime, sit back, take your Prozac, and let your kid have some fun for a change.

It's amazing to watch these parents act like the only thing that matters is that their little precious darling tried his or her best, then turn around and act like it's the end of the world when the ref makes a questionable call. Oftentimes it's hard to tell who's the kid and who's the adult!

Bob Uecker, I believe he missed the tag!

The Color Purple

———

For generations, teachers have used the color red to correct papers. Red was the color of choice for pragmatic reasons. Work, if completed in pen, is typically blue or black, and if done in pencil, dark gray. A contrasting color was needed so that students could easily see their mistakes and any comments, constructive or otherwise, the teacher may have had. Modern-day parents come along and are more concerned about their child's self-esteem than they are about them actually learning anything, and suddenly the color red becomes an evil lurking in the shadows, waiting to steal their child's innocence. Ah yes, the color purple is so much more appropriate. Have you ever read the book *The Color Purple* or seen the movie of the same name? Depressing as hell if you ask me.

I think George Carlin put it best in his 2008 HBO live stand-up comedy special, *It's Bad For Ya*, when he said:

> All this stupid bullshit that children have been so crippled by has grown out of something called the self-esteem movement. The self-esteem movement began in 1970 and I'm happy to say it has been a complete failure, because studies have repeatedly shown that having high self-esteem does not improve grades, it does not improve career achievement, it does not even lower the use of alcohol, and most certainly does not reduce the incidents of violence

of any sort, because, as it turns out, extremely aggressive, violent people think very highly of themselves! Imagine that, sociopath's have high self-esteem! Who would have thunk?[1]

George, you brilliant bastard, you!

I'll go a step further and say that not only has the feel-good, don't-hurt-anyone's-precious-feelings, self-esteem movement failed miserably, but it has actually had the opposite effect by contributing to the vices of today's society. In the grand scheme of this concept, children are taught that achievement is not important as long as they feel good about themselves or what they have done. And then when they grow up to be adults, we can't understand why they can't emotionally deal with being turned down after a job interview or, perhaps, being fired from their jobs. And we have to do studies to find out why the spike in depression is happening. Why kids are shooting other kids in our schools or, even worse, committing suicide because they are being teased and made fun of. Let's appoint another commission to do another study to come up with more statistics to figure this one out! It's no wonder we can't come close to solving *real* problems in this world when we're sitting around in serious debate as to why the color purple is so much more appropriate than red.

But *The Color Purple* was just the tip of the scholastic iceberg. It made political correctness look like a class four misdemeanor. It was the opening of the proverbial Pandora's Scooby Doo lunch box in terms of eradicating failure from our society, thus removing it from the dictionary altogether. You see, scholars *did* sit around in serious debate, and after much robust, intellectual discussion, they decided that fail, its past tense failed, and all other derivatives, (failure, failing) have no place in modern-day civilized society and should only be shamefully read about in history books. Therefore our astute, tenured scholars have replaced "failure" with "deferred success." No one fails anymore. Your success has simply been delayed a bit until you can get your shit together. We say, "Yes, little Bobby, because you screwed off this past year in school, your success has been deferred, and you will be spending next year repeating the second grade." Because the consequences have been so diluted in an effort not to hurt Bobby's feelings, it's hard to know if Bobby even understands what the consequences are. Does he understand that he will be spending an entire year repeating the same grade? Does he understand his friends are moving on without him? Fast forward twenty years, and Bobby will be hearing, "Bobby, your commission check will be late this month because of the deferred success of your sales quotas."

If you want to talk about a pristine, cream-of-the-crop example of what an overabundance of self-esteem can do to a child, just take a cold hard look at China's "one-child" policy that was enacted in 1980. In a culture where multiple generations often live under the same roof, typically in tight quarters, youngins, or should I say, the youngin, is the constant focus of attention by mom, dad, grandma, grandpa, and anyone else with an opium bed tucked in the corner.

While on a business trip to China in the early 2000s, a friend of mine met with a woman whose company provided behavioral health counseling for employees of Chinese companies. When my friend asked the woman what type of issues her counselors had to deal with (expecting to hear concerns like alcohol and drug abuse), she said that most of the counseling revolved around issues that arose out of China's one-child policy. Children were constantly told by everyone in the household how perfect and wonderful they were. Children were not accustomed to being yelled at or criticized, and as they grew, they could not handle rejection or the slightest hint of constructive criticism. They were not taught how to share things and were always receiving attention and affection without the need to reciprocate that very affection. As one can easily imagine, as these children grew, began dating, and entered the job market, they brought with them a whole host of unintended baggage, both professional and personal. Not to mention the societal side effects from this law—in a culture where the firstborn son is looked upon with the greatest of esteem, many female fetuses have been aborted over the last thirty years, causing a great imbalance in male-female ratios.

So if a world-class comedian can objectively see what the rest of us can't seem to figure out, then I will leave you with words from the brilliant Mr. Carlin who continued his monologue by stating, "A lot of these kids never get to hear the truth about themselves until they're in their twenties, when their boss calls them in and says, 'Bobby, clean the shit out of your desk and get the fuck out of here! You're a loser!'"

It would appear that in the not-too-distant future, the only precocious thing that Homo sapiens will be known for is narcissism.

Another sociopath in the making? I'm just saying!

Supersize Me!

A good friend of mine is a successful entrepreneur in the embroidery business. One day, a woman walked in and complained about the fit of her 4XL shirt that she purchased two days prior. She actually had the audacity to say, "It's not me that doesn't fit in the shirt, it's the shirt that doesn't fit on me!" My friend eloquently replied, "Ma'am, there's no such thing as a 5XL in that brand, but there is a thing called Weight Watchers!" After I was done laughing and wiping the tears from my eyes, my friend told me something so unbelievable that it made me question if he was telling the truth or not. Then I stopped and thought to myself: *We're talking about the human race here. Of course he's telling the truth!*

He said that large women in general were becoming self-conscious and embarrassed about ordering large sizes in clothing, so in order to help relieve large women of their reality, numerous major manufacturers and distributors of woman's clothing were skewing and reworking the sizing standards. L was still L, and XL was still XL, but apparently 2XL was the breaking point. Manufacturers, in their attempt to help women *feel* better about themselves, did away with 2XL and replaced it with 1XL. So let's see if you can follow me on this one.

The old system: S, M, L, XL, 2XL, 3XL, 4XL

The new system: S, M, L, XL, 1XL, 2XL, 3XL, 4XL

By adding the new 1XL in there, the old 2XL became the new 1XL, and everyone felt better about themselves. But it didn't stop there. The manufacturers, in their effort to help women psychologically lose even more weight, decided to do away with the designation L in all XL sizes and thus simplified the system even further: S, M, L, X, 1X, 2X, 3X, 4X. Unfortunately for all "well endowed" ladies out there, since not all manufacturers were on board with this new scheme, some using it and some not, the system became convoluted and just confused the hell out of everyone: customers, merchants, and suppliers alike. After a year or so of this little feel-good social experiment, the manufacturers went back to the old tried and true sizing system. I am willing to bet that in the not-too-distant future, the letter "X" will be the next new evil, pulling us down from our self-esteem chariot and preventing us from intellectual growth as individuals. Teachers will replace a red "X" with a purple ampersand, and the textile industry will replace "X" with an ampersand, so sizes will become S, M, L, &L, 1&L, 2&L, 3&L, 4&L. Doesn't that ampersand look so much softer, curvier, and sexier than that cold, hard, harsh, and insensitive X? I thought so!

It was bad enough when adults were fat, but then fat became the norm. Then fat became obese, and then obese became the norm. Now the norm is becoming a disease, and instead of doing something about it, we smother it in denial in classic Homo sapien form. The crime with all this is that we, the adults, the responsible ones, have allowed this "norm" to transgress to our children, and it is now perfectly acceptable for them to be obese. After all, it's not their fault that they eat garbage for breakfast, lunch, and dinner. It's not their fault that they sit on their asses and play video games all day long and don't get any exercise. It's not their fault that a significant portion of their daily intake of what few vegetables they do get consists of french fries and ketchup. And it's certainly not their fault that they take after their parents.

According to information from the American Heart Association:

Today, about one in three American kids and teens is overweight or obese, nearly triple the rate in 1963. Among children today, obesity is causing a broad range of health problems that previously weren't seen until adulthood. These include high blood pressure, type 2 diabetes and elevated blood cholesterol levels. There are also psychological effects: obese children are more prone to low self-esteem, negative body image and depression. And excess weight at young ages has been linked to higher and earlier death rates in adulthood.[1]

A growing number of children with high blood pressure and high cholesterol? Seriously? And we are standing around watching it happen, numb and clueless to the cause or the cure. I was reading a blog recently about obesity (because apparently I had way too much time on my hands). Some guy, when speaking counterpoint to exercise and metabolism, actually had the nerve to say, "If it was that easy, don't you think everyone would be thin?" No, they wouldn't! And unfortunately, that's the precise attitude that's gotten us to this point. You, mister blogger, are one of the millions who have accepted it as "the norm," thus making excuses for your obesity at every turn. You eat, drink, do what you want, and don't exercise. Then you jump up and run to your doctor whenever you feel like crap and have the nerve to turn around and bitch and complain about the high cost of health care!

I would agree: It's not always easy to lose weight. It takes a bit of effort, a bit of sacrifice, and a bit of discipline—there lies the root of the problem. There are certainly people out there who have certain biological conditions that make it difficult to lose weight, but these people should be the exception, not the norm, and we definitely should not be seeing this in children. When are "we" going to get back to the basics and start taking personal responsibility and accountability for "our" health, not letting that responsibility lie on the shoulders of our doctors or, God forbid, the government?

As I write this, the mayor of the Big Caramel-Covered Apple, Michael Bloomberg, in an effort to help fight obesity, is trying to place a ban on soft drinks in his city. No restaurant will serve any soda larger than sixteen ounces. One of his arguments, from a psychological standpoint, is that people have a tendency to finish whatever is in front of them so if you serve them smaller amounts, they will drink less. Seriously? Have you been to an all-you-can-eat buffet lately and seen the amount of shameful waste on plates that goes in the Dumpster? What about the amount of ice impacting the actual amount of soda in that sixteen-ounce serving? People will be ordering "no ice, please" and then Mr. B will have to impose a two-thirds ice-to-glass ratio ordinance. Just wait!

Yep, that's what I want in my life—people and parents can't take personal responsibility for their health or the health of their children, so "Big Brother" has to step in and do it for us, controlling more and more aspects of our lives, including what we can and can't eat when we pay hard-earned money at a restaurant. As if this ban is *really* going to impact an individual's personal habits when they get back home. You'd better go ahead and ban all buffets in town and the free-refill rule while you're at it.

An article on Today.com could not have put it more poignantly when it said, "New York City Mayor Michael Bloomberg stood firmly by his plan for a first-in-the-nation ban on large servings of soda and sugary drinks to fight obesity on Friday—even as the city celebrated National Doughnut Day."[2]

Richard Simmons, could you please pass the supersized number six combo with cheese-covered curly fries, a thirty-two-ounce Dr. Pepper, easy on the ice, and two chocolate chip cookies for my lunchtime dessert? Thanks. You tha man!

Imagine That!

As kids growing up in the late '60s and early '70s, our parents didn't want us inside, especially in the summertime. They would make us get the hell out of the house, into the one hundred degree heat, and we couldn't come back until we heard the dinner bell. (It was actually 112 degrees with the heat index, but we didn't know that because they hadn't invented the heat index back then, or if they did, they certainly didn't feel the need to advertise it. We all knew it was hot, so no one felt the need to walk around incessantly stating the obvious.) And we got out of the house gladly, just happy to be out of school for a little while.

My friends and I didn't have much in the way of entertainment, just the basics: some Matchbox Hot Wheel cars that we played with in the dirt, making roads and driveways by pushing the pine straw to the side of the flowerbeds. We had a football, a Frisbee, and Lawn Darts (that we tried to kill each other with). The most revered of all our possessions were our bicycles, which we would soup up by putting poker cards in the spokes or by painting red hot flames somewhere on the frame. We didn't have cell phones with GPS tracking capabilities so our moms could track our every step. We rarely came back to the house unless we needed something to drink, something to eat, or, depending on our age, if we got a bad bee sting, in which case our moms would kiss it, give us a glass of lemonade, smack us on our asses, and tell us to get back outside.

(I was over at a friend's house not too long ago, and his six-year-old got stung by a bee. Now I know a bee sting is a bit traumatic at that age, but you would have thought it was Armageddon. The child screamed bloody murder until his adrenaline began to wane, as he was exasperated by his mother's dramatic and overzealous bedside manner, all while the boy's father was on his iPad, feverishly researching anaphylactic shock.)

We spent our summers getting sweaty and dirty, rolling around in the grass, climbing trees, playing in the nearby woods, riding our bikes to the store to buy penny candies, going to the creek and torturing tadpoles, playing cops and robbers, cowboys and Indians, or just good guys and bad guys with sticks and throwing rocks at each other. Ah, those were the days! There was no one or nothing that kept us entertained except for our good old imagination.

Over the past decade, there have been numerous studies and an outpouring of articles written concerning the alarming decline in the creativity and imagination levels in children and even adults. One such article entitled "The Creativity Crisis," written by Po Bronson and Ashley Merryman, appeared in the July 10, 2010 issue of *Newsweek*. In the article, Po and Ashley reference a study conducted by Hyung Hee Kim, associate professor of educational psychology at the College of William & Mary. In the article, they state:

American creativity scores are falling. Kyung Hee Kim at the College of William & Mary discovered this in May, after analyzing almost 300,000 Torrance scores of children and adults. Kim found creativity scores had been steadily rising, just like IQ scores, until 1990. Since then, creativity scores have consistently inched downward. "It's very clear and the decrease is very significant," Kim says. "It is the scores of our younger children in America—from kindergarten through sixth grade—for whom the decline is most serious."[1]

["Dr. E. Paul Torrance developed the Torrance Test of Creative Thinking (TTCT) in 1966...The TTCT appears in almost forty different languages. Educators and corporate entities use and reference the TTCT more than any other creativity test in the world. The TTCT predicts creative achievement better than any other creativity test or divergent thinking test..."[2]—Kyung Hee Kim.]

So why is this happening, and why is it relevant? Depending on who you ask or what you read, there are a whole host of reasons for this decline. Kids watching way too much TV and/or playing way too many video games is certainly a good start. In regard to the former, the amount of TV they're watching is one issue, but let's also consider the quality of those programs. Reality TV, the staple crop of mainstream television today, is a melting pot of pestilence and mindless stupidity geared mostly around self-adulation and pointlessness (see chapter: Reality TV—Reality? Please!). At the other end of the media entertainment spectrum are the video games kids play. The graphics and special effects are so real, vivid, and unbelievably amazing (especially when you blow someone away with an AK-47) that it leaves little to the imagination. Anything that you possibly could or couldn't imagine is there for your viewing pleasure and requires no thought process on behalf of the unsuspecting viewer.

As a result of this extreme overstimulation (video games) or under-stimulation (TV), kids don't use their minds in the same creative way as in thousands of years past. The creative thinking process has virtually come to a halt. In the golden days of radio, before most households had televisions, entire families would gather around the radio and listen intently to shows like *The Green Hornet*,

Orson Welles Theater, The Shadow, Grand Ole Opry, Mickey Mouse Theater of the Air, The Lone Ranger and many others. Before television, radio inspired and demanded imagination and creative thought, but much of that has been lost with the advent of television. Now that the computer and digital imaging age is upon us, the creativity stream has been reduced to a trickle.

Other reasons for the significant decline in children's imagination and creativity levels would most certainly have to do with our lovely public education system. Most teachers today are stressed out enough by numerous aspects of their work environment: student-to-teacher ratios; disrespectful students; ADD and ADHD kids; behavioral issues impacting the demeanor and learning environment of the entire class; teacher's hands tied in terms of how to deal with inappropriate, disruptive, and even violent behavior; constantly worrying about who's going to bring the next gun to school; and dealing with overly protective and out-of-control parents. Don't forget the fact that these teachers are paid so well for putting up with all this crap when they are supposed to be teaching! And then we turn around and add insult to injury by taking away their creative freedom to teach by making them teach a standardized curriculum and holding them personally accountable for test score results in nationalized and regional testing platforms, which require educators to teach memorization of questions and answers like robots from a long lost civilization. And let's also consider the flip side of that coin—tenure. There are certainly many teachers who have earned their status and distinction. That being the case, let's let their achievements and accomplishments stand on their own. But also, let's face the cold hard truth: there are others who aren't good teachers. They're tired, frustrated, and burned-out, and their attitude not only shows, but is also reflected in their actions for all to see.

A good friend of mine became a physical education teacher in the Washington, DC, area. Fresh out of college, he was motivated and enthusiastic about working with junior high students and, hopefully, mentoring them and challenging them physically and intellectually. He was quickly disheartened. One story he would tell me was about one of his peers in the department who had been there for twenty-two years and was getting ready to retire. He smoked and was significantly overweight. Class after class, he would go to the gym, throw the kids some basketballs, sit in the bleachers, and read the newspaper. He didn't get "Teacher of the Year," and he didn't care because he had something better—tenure!

So again I ask: Why is all this relevant? Why is it important? I leave the answer to someone way smarter than I who once said, "Imagination is more important than knowledge." Einstein understood that it was his imagination and creativity that allowed him to think abstractly; that allowed him to think "outside the box"; that allowed him to dream up ideas, and concepts, and theories about space, time, light, and travel; that allowed him to write, and to change, the future. Einstein's traditional education brought him to a point where he understood the conventional thinking and ideas of the day, but in order to move forward and write the encyclopedias of the future, he had to think in ways that were not previously being construed. Quite simply, he had to – use his imagination!

Let's hope that one day our children will once again be able to dream the impossible dream and not just watch it on a video screen!

A Spoonful of Sugar Helps the Medicine Go Down

*M*r. Banks, Mary Poppins will be arriving soon, so let us prepare ourselves by examining some of the statistical facts of this household:

Autism: The Centers for Disease Control and Prevention (CDC) estimates that about 1 in 88 children has been identified with an autism spectrum disorder (ASD)...This new estimate marks a 23% increase since the last report...in 2009, and a 78% increase since the first report...in 2007.[1]

Obesity: The percentage of children aged 6-11 years in the United States who were obese increased from 7% in 1980 to nearly 18% in 2012. Similarly, the percentage of adolescents aged 12-19 years who were obese increased from 5% to nearly 21% over the same period.[2]

Diabetes: Diabetes is one of the most common chronic diseases in children and adolescents; about 151,000 people below the age of 20 years have diabetes...Each year, more than 13,000 young people are diagnosed with type 1 diabetes...Health care providers are finding more and more children with type 2 diabetes, a disease usually diagnosed in adults aged 40 years or older...The epidemics of obesity and the low level of physical activity among young people, as well as exposure to diabetes *in utero*, may be major contributions to the increase in type 2 diabetes during childhood and adolescence.[3]

Asthma: From 1980 to 1996, asthma period prevalence among children 0-17 years of age more than doubled, from 3.6% in 1980 to 7.5% at the peak of the trend in 1995. This prevalence remains at historically high levels...The factors driving this pattern are still not fully understood.[4]

ADHD: Approximately 9.5% or 5.4 million children 4-17 years of age had been diagnosed with ADHD, as of 2007, representing a 22% increase in four years.[5]

Developmental Disabilities: Prevalence of DDs (Developmental Disabilities) has increased 17.1%—that's about 1.8 million more children with DDs in 2006 to 2008 compared to a decade earlier.[6]

As identified in the source notes, all of the documented information above was taken directly from the Centers for Disease Control and Prevention (CDC) website, not the *National Enquirer.*

Now, I'm not a doctor, and I'm not going to pretend to be smarter than all the scientific research out there, but allow me to begin my discussion of the facts with a brief grassroots story of my mother and four of my five older siblings: A long time ago, my mother received a letter in the mail dated April 24, 1951, from the Department of the Navy, Bureau of Naval Personnel, which began, "Dear Mrs. Gerszewski: Pursuant to a request from your husband, passage has been booked for you and your four children in a Military Sea Transport Service Vessel scheduled to depart from Norfolk, Virginia, on 10 May 1951 for the Canal Zone."

My father was in the navy and had been transferred to Coco Solo, Panama. Dad went ahead to secure housing and such, as was often the custom in those days, while mom was left behind to tidy everything up on the home front. Although she was anticipating the move, upon receiving the confirmation letter, my mother had approximately fourteen days to pack up all the belongings and furnishings that were to be shipped to Panama, make arrangements for those items to be picked up and shipped, clean the house, find a realtor to rent the house, make arrangements to ship our Buick station wagon to Panama, pack carry-on luggage for a week's passage, forward the mail, and complete all the other stuff that was part of the stressful bliss that went along with moving to another part of the world. Mom got it done with the help of caring neighbors and friends who drove them to the pier and wished the five of them bon voyage!

The cruise took a little over a week, making a quick port of call in Puerto Rico on the way there. During that week, my mom did not have a TV, cable, Game Boy, Xbox, PlayStation, Nintendo, Wii, or iPhones to keep the little ones occupied. She did not have a cell phone, laptop, iPad, Internet, e-mail, Facebook, or Twitter to instantly keep in touch with the rest of the world. She took the kids for walks on deck (the two youngest ones were tethered by dog leashes and the four and five-year-old fended for themselves), played checkers with the older ones, and read to them in their tiny cabin or in the mess hall. Life was good! By today's standards, it is difficult and downright daunting to even imagine a mother of four kids, all of whom were under the age of five, accomplishing this without losing her mind, yet my mother did it. And I don't believe for one moment that my mother was unique in this regard. That's just what was required of parents to get the job done, and they did it to the best of their abilities with whatever tools they had available without griping or complaining about it. If you go back yet another fifty years to the turn of the twentieth century, parents did the same thing without electricity, indoor plumbing, an automobile, and, typically, with many more than four kids tugging at the apron strings. But even more amazing was the fact that none of the kids were autistic or diagnosed with Asperger's. None were depressed and saw a therapist on a routine basis. None were obese, had diabetes, high cholesterol, food allergies, or took any long-term prescription drugs. None suffered from asthma or ADHD and carried inhalers around with them everywhere they went. There were no "crack babies" or other *in utero* diseases, such as HIV, AIDS, STDs, hepatitis, or fetal alcohol syndrome. And the funny thing was none of the other neighborhood kids did either. (Actually there was one chubby kid who lived down the block named Arty.) They were just good, old-fashioned, healthy kids who drank water from the sink faucet, ate butter and lard, salted their food to taste, ate red meat, as well as a healthy amount of fresh vegetables every day, and they ran around outside in the fresh air, making the best of what they did or didn't have.

So why is it that with all the advances in modern medicine and all the resources and billions of dollars spent each year on medical research, not only can't we seem to fix the problems, but they are only getting worse? After all, the CDC states, "The reasons for the increase in the identified prevalence of ASDs (autism spectrum disorders) are not understood completely."[1] Also, "A major frustration in fighting asthma is the mystery of its development. It remains unknown why some people get the disease and others do not...The causes of asthma remain unclear and current research paints a complex picture."[4] "While ADHD can't be cured, it can be successfully managed."[5] Apparently childhood obesity can't be cured either since it is an epidemic on the rise that shows no signs of reversing course in the near future, even with the enormous health initiative going on in this country and around the world. These initiatives include changes like revamping the school lunch program; pressuring fast-food establishments to offer healthy alternatives; offering "organic food" or "health food" sections at more grocery stores; and our savior, Mayor Michael Bloomberg, banning sugary drinks.

Since modern science can't figure it out, allow me to be so bold as to offer some food for thought. Is it possible that the childhood diseases of today are by-products of our society? Is it possible that these are society-borne diseases that have spawned and continue to procreate from the blissful and cozy lifestyle we have created for ourselves? We have air pollutants, water contaminants, and frozen or fast-food meals void of any real nutritional substance shoved down our kids' throats just so we can get them to dance class or soccer practice on time. They only eat a couple fries because they are too busy playing with their Happy Meal toys, even though we have explained that ketchup and french fries are the primary source of their daily intake of vegetables. It's like the beginning of a bubonic plague all over again and we stand around blaming the rats and the fleas for the problem. If we spent some time addressing the root cause by cleaning up the garbage and the filth, the rodents would go away and so would the plague. Even Mary Poppins, in all her magic and wonder, would have a difficult time addressing the childhood concerns of today.

In 1976, air quality had become such a concern that the EPA (Environmental Protection Agency) established the AQI (Air Quality Index) to better track, document, and warn citizens of unhealthy air quality and the level of pollutants in the air. If bad enough, the AQI will recommend that we stay inside, where we may be subject to SBS (Sick Building Syndrome), yet another wonderful acronym spawned from the workings of modern-day society that we like to call progress. Because we all know that inhaling mold spores, mildew, and dust mites inside is so much healthier for us than the smog we breathe outside. The United States by no means has a monopoly on this concern as the UN (United Nations) and the WHO (World Health Organization) spend vast amounts of resources each year, financial and otherwise, researching the increasing concerns of pollutants and poor air quality worldwide.

What about water pollutants? We have known for decades that we should stop drinking large quantities of water from the faucet because health concerns may arise by doing so. In many countries, safe drinking water is a grave concern. Over the last thirty years or so, we have created the bottled water industry out of an alarming concern over the impurities in our tap water. But let's not fix the problem, let's just make a new law, or a new pill, or, in this case, a new industry to deal with it. And of course, we love bringing our bottled water to the beach where there may or may not be a swimming advisory posted, which prohibits us from swimming in the water because of a few hypodermic needles floating in the surf. There may also be a health risk of high bacteria levels, which are typically due to too much feces in the water or some other bacteria whose name I typically can't pronounce. And which government agency is responsible for telling the fish not to swim in the ocean, rivers, and lakes? Whoever it is, they're not doing a very good job at it because we routinely hear news stories and warnings concerning the high levels of mercury in certain types of seafood: "The Food and Drug Administration (FDA) and the Environmental Protection Agency (EPA) are advising women who may become pregnant, pregnant women, nursing mothers, and young children to avoid some types of fish and eat fish and shellfish that are lower in mercury."[7] Great. Now we have a fish consumption advisory to warn women who are even *thinking* about becoming pregnant to watch what fish they eat and how much.

For decades now, organizations like the American Heart Association and the American Cancer Institute have recommended, as part of a healthy diet and to help ward off serious debilitating and potentially deadly diseases, such as cancer and heart disease, we eat a healthy *daily* dose of five to seven servings of *fresh* fruits and vegetables (notice the emphasis on "daily" and "fresh"). This is not rocket science, and we have known the benefits of a healthy diet since before we were born. Eating something *fresh* and *real* has significant health benefits over something processed or frozen, heated in the microwave, or loaded with partially hydrogenated vegetable oils, high fructose corn syrup, preservatives, artificial flavoring, and coloring. God forbid our artificially flavored grape drink isn't purple. Better throw in some FD&C green #3, blue #1, and red #40 to ease our worried minds. We just can't seem to get enough of our artificial ingredients, can we?

An article on Forbes.com quoted several studies from the CDC and the US Department of Agriculture concerning the detriments of a diet loaded with processed sugar. The article, titled "What Eating Too Much Sugar Does to Your Brain," states:

> Overeating, poor memory formation, learning disorders, depression—all have been linked in recent research to the over-consumption of sugar...According to the US Department of Agriculture (USDA), the average American consumes 156 pounds of added sugar per year... The Center for Disease Control (CDC) puts the amount at 27.5 teaspoons of sugar a day per capita, which translates to 440 calories—nearly one quarter of a typical 2000 calorie a day diet...The problem is that we're chronically consuming much more added sugar in processed foods... Research indicates that a diet high in added sugar reduces the production of a brain chemical known as brain-derived neurotrophic factor (BDNF). Without BDNF, our brains can't form new memories and we can't learn (or remember) much of anything...which eventually leads to a host of other health problems. Once that happens, your brain and body are in a destructive cycle that's difficult if

not impossible to reverse...Research has also linked low BDNF levels to depression and dementia...We intuitively know that sugar and obesity are linked...What these and other studies strongly suggest is that most of us are seriously damaging ourselves with processed foods high in added sugar, and that the damage begins with our brains.[8]

But we know this. We know that too much sugar is bad for us and that we eat way too much of it. This is not some mysterious Masonic secret. The article even states, "We intuitively know that sugar and obesity are linked."

So what do we do about these societally bred health dilemmas that are now showing up in our children? Do we go back and deal with the polluted air situation? Airport oxygen bars are what all the cool kids are doing these days! Do we go back and clean up the contaminated water problem? Dasani, here we come! Do we bother to go out of our way to eat right and teach our children to do the same? Sunny Delight and Chocolate Cocoa Puffs—breakfast of champions! Do we get the appropriate amount of exercise? Wii Bowling! (There are actually a growing number of adults who consider Wii an acceptable alternative to traditional exercise. I would agree if you were eighty-eight years old and a nursing home resident, but not when you're eight.)

So what *do* we do? How does society deal with the dilemma at hand? We deal with it by taking the path of least resistance. We feed our children prescription drugs at an increasingly alarming rate. After all, why on earth would we consciously go out of our way to live a natural, healthy lifestyle that requires a little discipline and sacrifice when all we have to do is shove an Adderall down our kid's throat? Yes, we go running for the shelter of our mothers' little helper, as Mr. Jagger would say.

I teach children for a living, and I have seen the positive effects from kids taking these prescription drugs. I have also seen the horrible side effects and the negative impact of long-term use. The website Drugs.com (http://www.drugs.com/ritalin.html) states:

> Get emergency medical help if you have any of these signs of an allergic reaction to Ritalin; hives; difficulty breathing; swelling of your face, lips, tongue, or throat. Stop taking Ritalin and call your doctor at once if you have a serious side effect such as: fast, pounding, or uneven heartbeats; feeling like you may pass out; fever, sore throat, and headache with a severe blistering, peeling, and red skin rash; aggression, restlessness, hallucinations, unusual behavior, or motor tics (muscle twitches); easy bruising, purple spots on your skin; or, dangerously high blood pressure (severe headache, blurred vision, buzzing in your ears, anxiety, confusion, chest pains, shortness of breath, uneven heartbeats, seizure). Less serious Ritalin side effects may include: stomach pain, nausea, vomiting, loss of appetite; vision problems, dizziness, mild headache; sweating, mild skin rash; numbness, tingling, or cold feeling in your hands or feet; nervous feeling, sleep problems (insomnia); or, weight loss. This is not a complete list of side effects...[9]

Unusual behavior? What kind of side effect is that? I thought that's why the kid was on Ritalin to begin with! Restlessness? I thought that's what Ritalin was supposed to fix! And now that we have been turning our kids into zombies for the past several decades by feeding them Ritalin and Adderall at an alarming rate, how do we make amends for our childish over-prescription drug epidemic? We do it in classic Homo sapien style by inventing yet another disorder called sluggish cognitive tempo (SCT) for which we will invent yet another new drug to reverse the errors of our ways. If you have not yet heard of SCT and it sounds too absurd to be true, I suggest you Google it yourself.

And now the childhood, pop-a-prescription-drug epidemic has spilled over into our houses of higher education as more and more college students are using Adderall and Ritalin to help them focus better in their studies.

Mainstream society doesn't even try a holistic or homeopathic approach because it's too hard. The modern-day society we have created for ourselves doesn't allow time for it, so we simply take the path of least resistance, and, in the process, we teach our children that prescription drugs are just part of life. They are our friends (For some of us, they are our closest friends) and they will always be here for you no matter what challenges you face in life. You got the challenge. We got the pill!

"Mr. Banks, my summation of the facts concerning your children."

"Yes, Miss Poppins, what is it."

"Chim chiminy, chim chiminy, chim chim chiree! Or should I say, Supercallifragilisticexpialidocious!"

Whatcha Gonna Do When They Come for You?

March 2, 1932, *New York Times*, front page headline:

"Lindbergh Baby Kidnapped From Home Of Parents On Farm Near Princeton; Taken From Crib; Wide Search On"[1]

*T*he kidnapping of twenty-month-old Charles Augustus Lindbergh Jr., the son of Charles Lindbergh and his wife, Anne Morrow Lindbergh, from their home on the evening of March 1, 1932, was one of the most highly publicized crimes of the twentieth century. It was a sensationally sad story that polarized the nation for years. It spurred a massive manhunt of local, state, and even federal authorities, even though kidnapping at that time was not a federal crime. The body was found over two weeks later, partially buried by the side of the road, half eaten by wild animals. Cause of death: massive skull fracture. The investigation lasted over two years. A German immigrant, Bruno Richard Hauptmann was eventually arrested, tried, found guilty, and sent to the electric chair, four years and one month after the abduction. The case prompted congress to write and to pass the Federal Kidnapping Act, making it a federal crime to transport a kidnapping victim across state lines.[2]

Sadly, crimes against children are so commonplace today we barely take notice. We open up the paper or our laptops, read the horribly unimaginable and perverted news, pause for a moment to think how disgusting it is and how difficult it must be for the family, and then we move on. We turn the page or scroll down to the next pathetic story, take a sip of our Starbucks grande Caffe Misto, and look to see what other temporarily depressing news we can take in before we catch the 8:15 a.m. train into the city to put in our eight grueling hours.

The Lindbergh case, no doubt, brought both national and international attention because of the notoriety of the child's parents. Even so, there is no comparison to the sheer volume of child abuse and child murder cases that flood our daily headlines each and every day. Even more disturbing is not just the amount of child abuse going on today, but the type of child abuse. The old-fashioned beating-your-kids-to-a-pulp technique seems to pale in comparison to today's mainstream abuse: drowning your kids in the bathtub; strapping them in their car seats and driving the car into a lake; decapitation; dismembering them with an axe; locking them in the house and setting it on fire; waterboarding; locking them in cages and starving them to death. Then there's the good ol', make them watch as you shoot their mom in the head before turning the gun on them. Or better yet— make them watch as you shoot their mom in the head, then turn the gun on yourself and have them live that memory for the rest of their lives. Which is worse?

Below are just a few, I repeat, "a few," of the headlines from the summer and early fall of 2012 concerning the abduction, severe mistreatment, and/or murder of children, many at the hands of their own parents:

"Mom Accused of Killing Baby in Microwave"
hlntv.com, April 23, 2012

"Cops: Calif. Dad Killed Kids, Put Bodies in Trash"
newser.com, May 8, 2012

**"Florida Family Massacre: Tonya Thomas Shot Her
Kids 18 Times before Killing Herself, Reports Say"**
cbsnews.com, May 21, 2012

**"India: Father Kills Girl Baby;
Body Had Bite Marks, Cigarette Burns"**
lifenews.com, June 14, 2012

**"Father Kills Baby after Giving her
Formula Mixed with Vodka"**
dailymail.co.uk, June 15, 2012

"Mom Kills Kids by Throwing Them from Balcony"
nydailynews.com, June 25, 2012

**"4 charged with Running Florida Foster
Child Prostitution Ring"**
mcclatchydc.com, June 26, 2012

**"Dad Accused of Killing 3 Daughters Called
Mom and Said, 'You Can Come Home Now
Because I Killed the Kids', She Says"**
foxnews.com, July 12, 2012

**"Mom Trades Newborn for Pickup Truck,
Sells Truck for $800 and Some Meth"**
examiner.com, July 31, 2012

**"Tucson Police: Mother Kills 2 Children, Then Shoots
Herself (Children 17 mos & 4 yrs)"**
nbcnews.com, August 13, 2012

"Thai Mother Allegedly Kills, Eats Sons"
huffingtonpost.com, August 21, 2012

**"Mom Decapitated 2-Year-Old Child, Killed Self:
New Jersey Police"**
huffingtonpost.com, August 22, 2012

**"Father Killed 15-Week-Old Daughter
During Oral Rape"**
dailymail.co.uk, September 20, 2012

"China Cops: Man with Ax Kills 3 Kids at Day Care"
newser.com, September 21, 2012

"Mum 'Killed Five Babies' to Keep Standard of Living"
thelocal.de, September 27, 2012

**"Illinois Mom Stabbed Son and Girl
150 Times, Police Say"**
abcnews.go.com, November 01, 2012

"Mom Charged with Murder in Baby's Heroin Death"
myfoxphilly.com, November 09, 2012

"Mom Sells Daughter (13) as a Sex Slave for US $4"
bulawayo24.com, November 10, 2012

**"Father Kills Children after Mother's
'Midlife Crisis' Note"**
telegraph.co.uk, November 11, 2012

**"Mother Who Sold Her Two Daughters to a Pedophile
Finally Caught After 2 Years"**
yourblackworld.net, November 11, 2012

These horrible events are like car alarms going off in shopping mall parking lots. No one pays them any mind anymore. No one takes them seriously because it's expected and the norm.

"On January 13, 1996, nine-year-old Amber Hagerman was abducted while riding her bicycle in Arlington, Texas...Four days after the abduction, a man walking his dog found Amber's body in a storm drainage ditch."[3] Amber's abduction and murder are what began a grassroots crusade that eventually became known as an Amber Alert—a coordinated local, state, and federal effort to inform the public of a child abduction and pass on information in the hopes of quickly finding the child.

Unfortunately an Amber Alert is so common today that it barely raises an eyebrow. We hear it, see it, or read it; we think how horrible it is and then we move on. The kidnapping of a child today *should* be as polarizing as the Lindbergh case was eighty years ago, but it's not. It's almost as routine as turning on the car radio to hear the news itself that we barely seem to notice. Many of these crimes don't make it any further than your local news, and if they do, they're tucked away in the third section between the weather and the obituaries.

I started this chapter thinking it was going to be just another chapter about the deplorable decline of our species. As it turned out, it saddened me so much that I was ashamed I had to write it. These travesties toward children are single-handedly the greatest and gravest testament to the degeneration of our species. The headlines themselves speak volumes about the disintegration of our morals, beliefs, standards, actions, and the examples we set. If this is what we are willing to do to the most innocent of our species, what are we willing and capable of doing to the rest of humanity?

My favorite headline from the summer of 2012:

"Experts: Moms Who Kill Kids Often Driven by Love"
floridatoday.com, May 16, 2012

Kind of warms your heart, doesn't it?

Section 2:

The Rise of the Machines

Your Pubes Are Showing

So we've survived our young impressionable years without adding to the childhood mortality rate. Our peers have laid down the societal ground rules and planted the seeds of our evolution in their footsteps. We have not been spanked, disciplined, scolded, or reprimanded in any meaningful way, and if we have, we're probably one of the statistics from the previous chapter. We are no longer put in time-out. We have never been told anything negative about ourselves and only know that everything we do is amazingly wonderful, regardless. We have never been exposed to rejection or loss of any kind and are emotionally sheltered from anything negative or bad regardless of the reality of the situation. We are pumped so full of self-esteem that we can do no wrong, and it will be years before reality knocks us off our throne. We are raised by day cares, babysitters, and nannies. We are allowed to watch pretty much anything we want on TV or on the Internet with little or no supervision. Often we are encouraged to watch TV or a computer monitor just to keep us quiet for a while. We are spoiled rotten, unappreciative, and disrespectful. Our imagination and IQ levels continue to decline year after year. We have horrible fast-food diets filled with everything artificial and devoid of any real nutritional substance. We don't exercise, as well, and we are obese and infected with an entire host of adult onset diseases for which we are overmedicated.

And now we reach puberty! And what do we have here? A recipe for disaster. We now reach the point in our young lives that matters the most, the time when we begin to test our freedoms with caution and uncertainty. We begin to think independently and formulate opinions about the world around us. We break away, rebel, and question authority because we have all the answers. We begin to experiment with drugs and alcohol. We experience maddening, uncontrollable hormones and sexuality. We begin to desire things of our own that have previously always been provided for, or denied, us.

Yes, the modern-day Homo sapien is now entering a volatile period where the influences from his or her childhood have set the standard, and the precedent, of what is acceptable, what is expected, and what is the norm.

Sigmund Freud once said, "Children are completely egoistic; they feel their needs intensely and strive ruthlessly to satisfy them."[1] You throw in a healthy amount of narcissistic, overprotective, drug-addicted, non-disciplined spoilage into the mix, forget to stir the pot over the last several decades, and what do you have? A recipe for a changing society that is headed over the proverbial cliff.

And so, without further ado, let us see how the adolescent stage of modern-day human evolution will be impacted by the influence and examples of our childhood upbringing.

Can You Hear Me Now?

No, I'm afraid I can't hear you now. And if I could, there's a good chance I wouldn't be able to understand your mumbling, incoherent colloquialisms. I wouldn't understand your fluent valley girl, your abstract slang, your mysterious chitchat, your verbal acronyms, your nouveau idioms, your inner-city jive, your Ebonics, your extreme southern drawl, your country boy redneck, your geographically challenged vernacular, your I-don't-give-a-shit attitude and figure of speech. And even if I could read lips, it would be nearly impossible to discern because you're not making eye contact with me and with your head turned like that, I can't see your lips clearly. Are you talking to me or someone else? Oh, I'm sorry. I didn't see the Bluetooth sticking out of your ear. It's as if you're a drunken, rambling, mental health patient whose dialect I can't comprehend. But you're not. You're my neighbor on Main Street, USA. So to answer your question: no, I can't hear you now and getting an upgrade to your service isn't going to do any good either.

The 1900 census of the United States listed my great-grand-parents as having one of the largest families in America, with twenty children born to the same mother and father (Yes, that's correct and not a typo—the "same" mother and father). One of their daughters, Katherine, or Katie as she was commonly known, was born deaf. As a result, Mom, Dad, and all the other seventeen children (two of the twenty died in infancy) learned sign language so that *everyone* could communicate with her. In a day and time when their four-room farmhouse in rural South Dakota had no electricity, no indoor running water, and the family had no automobile to get them around, learning sign language for each and every family member must have been an exasperating labor of love. But they did it out of a sense of family, unconditional love, and a basic understanding that clear and coherent communication was essential to keep the 110 acres tilled, harvested, and everything humming along smoothly. Today, even with the cushy lifestyle we enjoy, it's hard to imagine a family with four kids, not to mention ten or twenty, finding the time to fit sign language classes into everyone's schedule. We just ship the deaf-mute off to a special school or a special work environment where they will "fit in."

Not too long ago, I was at an annual awards dinner for work. One of the couples I shared a table with brought their fifteen-year-old Goth daughter along; and she, for company, brought along her smartphone, which was the only thing smart about her. Sitting next to her, I tried to engage in casual conversation, asking questions like "What school do you go to?" "What subjects are you interested in?" "Play any sports?" "What kind of music do you like to listen to?" and "What do you want to do when you graduate?" I was obviously being a pesky geezer, and she was obviously more interested in sexting or whatever she was doing because I got a one or two word answer, and then she went right back to her phone, sometimes without even making eye contact. And if her lack of communication wasn't bad enough, her nonexistent interpersonal communication skills were atrocious and annoying. But this is not any big secret or revelation as it is the norm of today's youth. I think Tommy Lee Jones put it best in his portrayal of Ed Tom Bell, the aging sheriff, in the Coen Brothers movie *No Country for Old Men*. The sheriff was having coffee with a fellow law enforcement officer, and the two of them were discussing the younger generation and how they are becoming the dregs of society. At one point in the conversation, in his distinct southern drawl, the sheriff so eloquently points out, "I think once you quit hearin 'sir' and 'ma'am,' the rest is soon to faller."

People used to call each other on the rotary phone to catch up and see how the other was doing. But who needs that when we have Facebook to keep track of what Aunt Rose had for breakfast while visiting the grandkids in Toledo? No, calling someone is too much of an inconvenience and speed dial takes way too much time, so let's just text, preferably while driving. Yes, let's reduce the English language to a bunch of acronyms and mumbling in 144 characters or less: omg, lol, wtf, r u cra z? ygg, lmao, btw, ty, gtg, ttyl, lyl, bff, xoxo.

It's no wonder no one writes anymore because it takes way too long, and who has time for that? Even the once a year Christmas card has transgressed into a cheesy mass-produced by-product of commercialization, pointing out every nuance of one's pathetic life that I have already read about on Facebook, such as the unbridled excitement from renting a Prius during one's summer vacation. Even as I type, Christmas cards are evolving into the next level of complacency. No more handwritten letters, no more cheesy mass-produced letters, simply a glossy card on which is embossed a family photo that simply states an ambiguous "Happy Holidays," and if we're lucky, a genuine handwritten cursive signature at the bottom. If we're lucky! I guess I shouldn't complain as this is personally preferably over most heinous mass-produced Christmas letters.

I was shocked to learn recently that cursive writing is no longer being taught in many school municipalities around the country. Proponents of not teaching cursive will tell us we live in the computer age, nothing other than our signature is written in this antiquated cursive anymore, and everything is typed on a keyboard. So what do we do when the next hurricane or major snow storm rolls through, knocking out the power? Heaven forbid we find ourselves without computers or smartphones for a week or two. What happens if we're studying history and come across a handwritten letter that we need to decipher or identify whose signature is at the bottom? Forget about going to Washington, DC, to visit the National Archives to read the original Declaration of Independence, the Constitution, or the Bill of Rights. Ain't gonna happen. You will have to request a printed version for anyone left on the planet that might have an interest in reading them in the first place. And even if you can read them, what's the chance you will be able to understand what you're reading because it's written in that mumbo jumbo, Old English, Shakespearian-type dialect? I give it another fifty years or so, and universities will be offering master's degrees in cursive. Like hieroglyphics, it will be a highly specialized degree in archeology, and the professors of this study will be known as cursiveologists. You think that's too far-fetched? Many people and institutions of higher education in this country have already recognized and legitimized Ebonics as an official, separate language. The problem has gotten so bad that in recent years, the FBI, DEA, and several other government agencies have been actively engaged in hiring individuals who are fluent in Ebonics. It's like the government hiring Native Americans during World War I, World War II, and Korea to be code talkers, sending radio transmissions in their native tongue so the enemy has no idea what we're talking about. The only problem today is we're not at war with ourselves. Or are we? Ebonics is just another lowering of the standards because we can't talk good English!

I'm not sure why not teaching cursive in school is so surprising to me. I suppose it's because I think of it as a basic fundamental aspect of learning and life—reading, writing, and arithmetic. Perhaps we should consider revising it to reading, printing, and arithmetic. And then in another fifty years or so we can change it to sound it out, print the pretty word, count on your fingers.

We can't even decide on an official language in the good ol' United States of America. It's one thing to have multilingual signs and information available in certain geographical areas in this country or at international points of travel, such as airports and train stations, but to turn around and suggest that we shouldn't have an official language because we are "the great melting pot" is unintelligible to me. I think that being the great melting pot is even more reason why we should have an official common language. Establishing a common language and having a clear and coherent understanding of that language is one of the fundamental cornerstones of any civilized society. Without it, one is most certainly destined to fail.

A friend of mine and I were recently debating this very point. He pointed out that people of most, if not all, European countries speak numerous languages. I replied that it was true that an overwhelming majority of people in European countries are multilingual and that the situation arose out of a significant change in countries' borders over the years along with the close proximity of these countries to each other. As a result, one needed to learn their neighboring countries' languages in order to effectively do business with them. It would be as if every state in the United States spoke a different language, and if you wanted to travel, conduct commerce, or simply had friends in other states, it would necessitate learning other languages at an early age. I also pointed out that even though most people in Europe were multilingual, most countries had an official language. My friend then noted that Canada is a bilingual country. I said that was *great* for Canada! Time and events in history have dictated that to be the most appropriate linguistic situation for Canada. But I also pointed out that French and English were, in fact, the official languages of Canada, and, more importantly, the people of Canada were, for the most part, quite articulate in their use of both French and English. You could go to Vancouver or Montreal and understand what everyone was saying. The Canadians use of those two languages was not disintegrating into a form of Ebonics, slang, or valley girl to the point where Canadians were validating and justifying the use of other lingual morphisms. In conclusion, I told my friend that I was all for teaching American kids foreign languages. I think all kids should be bilingual or trilingual, I said, simply from the standpoint that education will hopefully increase their cultural awareness and geographic curiosity. But let's start by learning how to speak proper English first and stop using it as an excuse to legitimize and justify other subtexts of English just because we are too ignorant to speak it properly in the first place!

If the phasing out of cursive isn't bad enough, the advancement of the computer and technological age have brought with it a whole host of seemingly harmless communicable problems and addictions that everyone simply writes off as "change." We are addicted to texting, the incessant need for information *now*, and the incessant need to pass that information on as soon as we hear it without confirming its validity. (We have all been guilty, at one time or another, of forwarding a picture to someone that we thought was real, only to find out it was photoshopped, or passing along information that was not accurate simply because we *needed* to share it with someone in the moment.) What about vehicular death by texting or vehicular death by cell phone? The availability of Internet porn to young people; sexting, teens sending their boyfriends or girlfriends naked pictures and videos of themselves; videotaping your most intimate moments for the personal and private pleasure of you and your partner, only to find out the video went viral when you became ex-partners; Internet pedophiles (we have made pedophiles' jobs so much easier to the point that many law enforcement agencies have had to hire people or, in some instances, entire departments to hunt down and track pedophiles by posing as kids on the Internet); identity theft; or addiction to social media and video games—the list goes on!

Yes, for every solution our new technology brings, it brings problems tenfold. This is happening so fast, we are not capable of dealing with it in a socially responsible manner. In the meantime, kids, and even some adults, are losing the ability to simply communicate with one another. No one has social skills anymore, and no one cares as long as they make it to the next level of *God of War: Ascension.* No interpersonal communication skills, no basic manners, no patience, no problem-solving skills, no respect, no common sense or the ability to think abstractly. So no, I can't hear you now!

I said...What? No, I said I can't...Hello? What did you say? Hello? Your phone's a piece of...What? Hello?

Call lost!

Civilization lost!

Mankind lost!

Can you hear me now?

Are You Smarter Than A Fifth Grader?

---

re *you* smarter than a fifth grader? No, most of us aren't. If we were, there wouldn't be a show called *Are You Smarter Than a Fifth Grader?* Hence the following transcript:

Jeff Foxworthy: Pick another subject, and let's go to two thousand.

Jennifer: All right, let's go with uh, second grade measurements.

Jeff: Jennifer, the two-thousand-dollar question is: If Jacob stands on Spencer's shoulders, they are two and a half yards high. How many feet is that?

Jennifer: Um, two and a half yards, and I took a chemistry class too, and that was one of the...

Jeff: You learned this in chemistry class. Where did you go to school?

Jennifer: In Texas.

Jeff: It sounds like you were homeschooled and you were there by yourself.

Jennifer: There's 352 feet in a yard!

Jeff: The basic question here really is how many feet are in two and a half yards?

Jennifer: Right.

Jeff: How many feet are in one yard seems to be the big stumbling block. Does *three* ring any kind of a bell? You had 352, which is close to the days in a year.

Jennifer: My name is Jennifer, and I learned something. I am not smarter than a fifth grader.[1]

I paraphrased the dialogue a bit to spare you the agony of reading the slow demise of the human race, but please feel free to witness it in its entirety on YouTube. And that was just the $2,000 question!

Watching that video, I could not help but be reminded of the scene from the futuristic movie *Idiocracy* where the main character, Joe, played by Luke Wilson, is sent to prison and has to take an aptitude test to determine his job skills, or as the guard puts it, "OK, sir, this is to figure out what your aptitude's good at and get you a jail job while you're being a particular individual in jail." One of the questions that Joe is asked on the test is, "If you have one bucket that holds two gallons and another bucket that holds five gallons, how many buckets do you have?" Joe, being the smartest man on the planet in the year 2505, correctly answers the question. Oh, by the way, the answer is two!

I have always insisted that *Idiocracy*, a futuristic thriller of the dumbing down of the human race, should be in the horror section of our local video stores instead of the comedy section, but recently, a friend of mine brought to my attention the fact that, "It's already happening and really belongs in the documentary section." *Idiocracy* begins with a picture of earth from outer space. As the camera slowly zooms in on planet Earth, the narrator begins:

As the twenty-first century began, human evolution was at a turning point. Natural selection, the process by which the strongest, the smartest, the fastest reproduce in greater numbers than the rest, a process which had once favored the noblest traits of man (as the dialogue continues, the picture of Earth is overlaid with pictures of Einstein, Beethoven, Darwin, Botticelli's *The Birth of Venus,* and da Vinci's *Vitruvian Man*) now began to favor different traits (now overlaid with pictures of professional wrestlers and scantily clad women). Most science fiction of the day predicted a future that was more civilized and more intelligent, but as time went on, things seemed to be heading in the opposite direction: a dumbing down. How did this happen? Evolution does not necessarily reward intelligence. With no natural predators to thin the herd, it began to simply reward those who reproduced the most and left the intelligent to become an endangered species.

Mike Judge and Etan Cohen, the writers of *Idiocracy,* must be clairvoyant, or maybe they're just looking at the world objectively with their eyes wide open, because there was a recent article in the Huffington Post titled "People Getting Dumber? Human Intelligence Has Declined Since Victorian Era, Research Suggests." The article went on to say:

Our technology may be getting smarter, but a provocative new study suggests human intelligence is on the decline. In fact, it indicates that Westerners have lost 14 IQ points on average since the Victorian Era. What exactly explains this decline? Study coauthor, Dr. Jan te Nijenhuis, professor of work and organizational psychology at the University of Amsterdam, points to the fact that women of high intelligence tend to have fewer children than do women of lower intelligence. This negative association between IQ and fertility has been demonstrated time and again in research over the last century.[2]

Another Huffington story boasts, "Fifty-seven percent of recent mothers without a high school diploma were unmarried compared to nine percent of recent mothers with a bachelor's degree or higher. Sixty-nine percent of recent mothers (who) came from households with incomes with $10,000, in contrast to nine percent of recent mothers with households earning $200,000 or more."[3]

So, let me see if I got this straight. The earth has warmed roughly 1.5 degrees Fahrenheit over the last one hundred years, and everyone is in a hissy fit over it. Human intelligence has cooled fourteen IQ points over the last 150 years or so, and no one seems to care. Could the cooling of intelligence explain the rise in temperatures? I'm just asking!

There are numerous angles of attack we could take in determining the culprit of this intellectual demise. Some would say that the high school dropout rate is a significant factor. I would say that the dropout rate is one of the last dominos to fall. It is not the cause, but the effect of many societal idiocracies, such as less and less oversight and supervision of kids; teens having babies; burned-out teachers who are sick and tired of the system, but they aren't worried because they have tenure; increased behavioral issues and health concerns; the medication of children on a level never before seen in human history; the decline of imagination levels in children; and the fact that standardized test requirements are being compromised to ensure that no child is left behind. You add all this up, and it's easy to see why public education isn't what it used to be.

Allow me to use an analogy of health care to further explain. People should be their own first line of defense in caring for themselves and only run to their doctor when things get bad, but that's not how it typically works. People usually eat, drink, and behave like they want, and then run to their doctors every time they feel like crap, expecting the doc to have some miracle cure. Using this analogy, the first line of intellectual defense should be a good, loving, supportive, and disciplined home life. Then students can prosper in academics and extracurricular activities. But to many parents, educating their children is the school's job. Kids can run amuck at home with little supervision or discipline, then the parents expect the burned-out teachers to perform miracles. It doesn't work like that, and it's amazing that many parents don't get it.

Proponents of our public education system will argue that the high school dropout rate has decreased over the last couple decades. That being the case, I would question the quality of the public education children are getting today as opposed to forty or fifty years ago. It seems we have simply traded quality for quantity just so we can meet some quota and look good on paper. And even with the decline in high school dropout rates, the numbers are still staggering:

- Number of high school students who drop out each day—8,300[4]

- Total number of high school dropouts annually—3,030,000[4]

- Percent of all dropouts that happen in the ninth grade—36%[4]

- Percent of students in the largest 50 US cities that graduate high school— 59%[4]

- Percentage of US crimes committed by a high school dropout—75%[4]

- Percent of black dropouts that have spent time in prison—60%[4]

- Percentage of Hispanic dropouts that were due to a pregnancy—41%[4]

- Percent of US jobs a high school dropout is not eligible for—90%[4]

So if the fifth graders ain't as smart as they used to be, and the adults, on average, ain't as smart as the fifth graders, and if you have the ability to convert two and a half yards into feet, then it's not rocket science to come up with the educated hypothesis that we're doomed!

The Wikipedia page for *Idiocracy* describes the movie as:

The film tells the story of two ordinary people from the present who take part in a top-secret military hibernation experiment, only to be awaken 500 years in the future in a dystopian society full of extremely stupid people. Advertising, commercialism, and cultural anti-intellectualism have run rampant and dysgenic pressure has resulted in a uniformly unthinking society devoid of intellectual curiosity, social responsibility, and coherent notions of justice and human rights.[5]

Take a look around us, ladies and gentlemen. We don't have to wait five hundred years because it's already happening. As I mentioned earlier, the movie is not a comedy anymore. It's a documentary and a horror film, and if we open our eyes and take a good look around, we won't need a fifth grader to tell us it's so!

She Loves Me—She Loves Me Not

"**I** love you! I love you! I love you!" When my fifteen-year-old son started saying that to his first real girlfriend ten to twenty times a day, I told him to knock it off, and he knew I meant it. He was saying it because all his friends were saying it. It was all the rage with the cool kids—the latest, greatest hormone-induced, cultural enigma sweeping his generation, bred from the cultural paradox that they don't know what "love" is anymore. And why should they know what it is when the only thing many of them are surrounded by are broken homes with working, single parents with visitation rights, and no true father figure or role model to emulate? It's no wonder they gravitate to people, substances, events, and a superficial culture that fills that emotional void for them.

My mother, being born and raised along the Yellowstone River in rural eastern Montana during the 1920s and 1930s, never once told me, or any of her other five children as far as I know, that she loved us. Probably because it was never said in her household growing up with eight other siblings and a loving mother and father. And yet, in the forty years that she and I walked this planet together, there was never, ever any doubt in my mind that she didn't love me unconditionally. That's because actions spoke louder than words. There was no need to walk around incessantly repeating "I love you" over and over again, like some hourly affirmation that needed to be constantly stated and reinforced because there was nothing else of substance to show for it.

The status quo relationships of today are, for the most part, superficial, pretentious, and devoid of any substance or understanding of what it means to be in a serious relationship. It's a no-brainer that teens don't learn how to work through problems or differences that arise because they haven't been taught those skills, and even if they have, it's difficult to apply them to a baseless relationship. Today's kids fall in love (infatuation) one day, make love (have casual sex) the next day, and then break up tomorrow by texting to let the other one know how much they hate him or her and that they posted their sex tape on Facebook and YouTube. Not only is this just a pathetic way of conducting themselves, especially when it comes to intimacy, but it's an incredulous cop-out. Teens don't have the guts or the communication skills required to discuss and work through problems face-to-face or, at the very least, tell the individual in person how they are feeling. And why should they when we, the adults, the responsible ones, have led by our own example? Nothing is sacred anymore. Instead it's all about whatever makes you happy in the moment.

Several years ago, a close friend of mine who works in a hair salon told me she was cutting a woman's hair one day, and the customer was chatting away in a classic woman-to-woman conversation about her daughter's upcoming wedding. During the course of the conversation, the woman said that her daughter was "getting married for the first time." The statement went in one ear, out the other, and then was sucked back into my friend's cerebral cortex. *"Getting married for the first time?" What an odd thing to say*, my friend thought to herself. I'm sure the woman probably didn't even realize what she said. It just slipped out—a subconscious Freudian slip of the truth, an emancipation proclamation of the times!

I'm sure one could easily make the argument that the only reason so few people got a divorce back in the day was because it wasn't socially acceptable, it was frowned upon, and anyone who sought out a divorce, particularly if you were a woman, was shunned and scorned. If that's the case, then today we have come full circle—not only is divorce perfectly acceptable, it's expected, and it's changing the face of mankind. Today getting a divorce is no longer the exception to the rule; it *is* the rule and the societal expectation.

Once upon a time not too terribly long ago when men were men, a man would not think to ask a woman's hand in marriage before proving himself financially or, at the very least, being well established on his career path. Then and only then would he go and ask the father of his bride-to-be for the daughter's hand in marriage. Even then, the man typically did that only after a lengthy courtship to see if, in fact, the two were compatible, not just experiencing spontaneous infatuation that the modern-day youth mistakes for love. The men of that long forgotten era of sixty to seventy years ago would open doors for women, pull their chairs out for them, they would not sit until their female companions were seated, they would help a woman with her coat, and they took their hats off when they came inside. Those clearly defined roles and responsibilities were performed simply out of common courtesy for the opposite sex, which was the societal norm. Then came the baby boomers who decided that their parents had no clue how to raise kids; the feminist movement, which told women to burn their bras; and sociologists, who said it was bad for kids to see their parents fighting, and it was much better for the kids if the parents divorced. And now, young males have no clue what their roles and responsibilities in relationships should be. They have no clue how to treat a young woman. It's just a here-today-gone-tomorrow, add-water-and-microwave-for-two-minutes kind of relationship. They have no clue what a commitment is and how much hard work and mutual respect goes into a healthy relationship. Yes, thanks to the boomer, the feminist, and the progressive sociologist, traditional wedding vows are taking on a whole new meaning. Like many things in modern-day society, if we don't agree, we simply change or rewrite them, or we just adapt them to whatever meaning suits us in the moment.

The following vows are what I like to refer to as "The Modern-Day, For Better or Worse, Take It or Leave It, She Loves Me, She Loves Me Not, Wedding Vows." They are real-life observations and experiences from a friend of mine who is now enjoying his retirement after thirty-five plus years of practicing family law and foster care parenting.

"I, Laura, take you, Luke, to be my lawfully wedded husband, to have and to hold from this day forward, for better (I'm sure that marriage is going to change you, and if you *really* love me, you will stop all your irritating habits, like leaving the toilet seat up. You will change your mind and *will* want children after all, and if not, then I will conveniently forget to take my birth control pill. You *will* stop ogling other women, and if you don't, then I will be entitled to get a divorce.)

or worse (Except I really don't expect things to get worse, and if they do, it will be your fault because of *your* lack of communication skills, appreciation, and empathy. If you leave me alone one too many nights to go out with your buddies, then I will be entitled to get a divorce.)

for richer (Once you get your GED, I expect you to start making one hundred grand a year, and buy me that brand new Ford Mustang I always wanted so I can show it off to all my friends with our new baby that you never wanted. If you don't, I will be entitled to get a divorce.)

for poorer (Don't even think of losing your job, regardless of the economy or the job market, because I cannot live on unemployment and food stamps since I don't know how to deal with that. I was always brought up to believe that my life would be a pristine bubble of love and happiness. Besides, I'm pregnant again, and if we are poorer, I will be entitled to get a divorce.)

in sickness (Like a cold or the flu is fine, but if you get some debilitating disease that requires round-the-clock care, forget it. And don't even think about losing a limb in Afghanistan or becoming significantly handicapped in a horrific car accident that wasn't your fault because I didn't bank on that. If you do, I will be entitled to get a divorce.)

and in health (Don't get old and wrinkly, stop exercising, or become morbidly obese, because if you do, I will be entitled to get a divorce.)

to love (Like, you know, I love you now, but if my heart stops fluttering every time you walk by, and you are no longer as exciting to me as my sharply dressed, meticulously groomed, personal trainer coworker that I have to look at every day, and he's as lonely as I am because you're off working double shifts to make ends meet because I'm pregnant again, then of course, I will be entitled to get a divorce.)

and to cherish (Unless you get fat and ugly, or don't shave on the weekends, or eat garlic pizzas when you know I'm horny, or chew your fingernails and crack your knuckles, or continue to do any of the other irritating things that you know I despise about you, then I will be entitled to get a divorce.)

from this day forward until death do us part (Or at least until I file for divorce and the prenup kicks in.)."

Yes, the modern-day interpretation of traditional wedding vows are designed to suit our needs of the moment because we never taught our kids what was really important in life and how difficult it is at times to keep a committed relationship going.

Sometime back in the '90s, I was watching Letterman or Leno (I can't remember which) do his monologue and he was talking about a current event story about an Australian couple that was getting a divorce and fighting over custody of frozen embryos. The host said that the judge had awarded the couple joint custody of the embryos. The punch line was, "I guess that means he gets to keep them in his freezer on weekends!" That seemingly innocuous joke has stuck with me all these years as quite hilarious and profoundly sad at the same time. The fact that we have created these types of societal and moral dilemmas, as if we have nothing of greater importance to worry about, is very sad. It's bad enough when kids are the pawns in the game of divorce, but now an embryo is becoming the game piece of choice.

Ask any child of divorce what he or she really, really wishes for, and an overwhelming majority of them will tell you they just want their parents back together again. They don't want to deal with all the bullshit and drama. They don't want to have to deal with mom's new boyfriend or dad's new trophy wife. They don't want to spend one weekend here and one weekend there. They don't want to be caught in a tug-of-war of emotions, finger-pointing, and insider trading. No, they just want to be a family again, even if that means Mom and Dad arguing every once in a while, which will unknowingly teach them that life is not perfect, things do get difficult from time to time, and it takes a tremendous amount of patience and mutual respect to make things work. You can't just jump overboard every time life gets tough. Is that too much to ask? Don't answer that. It was, well, you know, rhetorical.

"Welcome to Costco, I love you."

—*Idiocracy*, the movie.

Please Pass the Roll Model—Pleeeese!

*I*don't remember where I was the moment I heard that Kurt Cobain had just blown his head off. It wasn't a moment so debilitating for me that I would remember where I was and what I was doing, such as when the World Trade Center came down, the modern-day equivalent of remembering where you were when you learned Kennedy had been shot. The closest empathy I could conjure concerning the whole Kurt Cobain incident was remembering where I was when I heard John Bonham had choked to death on his own vomit. I was a horny nineteen-year-old college student and Led Zeppelin fanatic, driving through a residential neighborhood in Danville, Virginia. I heard it on the AM/FM radio of my Chevy Vega, and I was so stunned that I pulled over and sat on the side of the road for a few minutes. No cell phone to text anyone the news. But after a few minutes, I gathered my thoughts, got back on the road, and got on with my life. I never thought of Bonzo as a role model, just an amazingly talented percussionist who I couldn't get enough of at the time. By contrast, when Kurt Cobain killed himself, many of his fans openly wept in the streets, professing him to be a god. Seriously? A god? I guess in today's pop culture world, writing and recording some pretty good music *is* the modern-day equivalent of instantly curing a man of leprosy.

Role models used to be individuals who contributed something positive and worthwhile to their family and society as a whole. Amazing people like, oh, I don't know, Mom or Dad! Believe it or not, the most revered role model in the eyes of a kid *is* a really cool mom or dad. But with roughly 25 million American kids being raised in single-parent homes,[1] and most of those parents often working to make ends meet, it's difficult to always be there for them no matter how good of a parent you are. And when they *are* home with their children, they're busy attending to the necessities like making dinner, washing clothes, packing lunch for tomorrow, helping with homework, and running for groceries or to soccer and dance classes, all while exhausted, stressed out, and on edge. Under these circumstances, even with the best of intentions, it's tough to be a cool, positive role model for your kid day in and day out.

Statistics posted on the government website Child States.gov (www.childstats.gov) paint a depressing and pathetic picture of today's modern-day family unit: "The composition of families is dynamic and has implications for critical parental and economic resources. A long-term shift in family composition has decreased the share of children living with two married parents, while single-parent households have become more common for children."[1] The site continues by stating:

- Sixty-four percent of children ages 0–17 lived with two married parents in 2012, down from 77 percent in 1980.[1] [I would like to stop here for a moment so I can translate those percentages into some individual figures. There are 70 million children in this age bracket. Sixty-four percent of these kids live with two parents who are married to each other. That means that 36 percent of US kids live in one-parent, foster parent, or no-parent households, and 36 percent of 70 million kids is 25.2 million kids. Roughly 25 million US kids between the ages of newborn to seventeen live in a single-parent or no-parent home.]

- In 2012, 24 percent of children lived with only their mothers, 4 percent lived with only their fathers, and 4 percent lived with neither of their parents.[1]

- Seventy-four percent of White, non-Hispanic, 59 percent of Hispanic, and 33 percent of Black children lived with two married parents in 2012.[1]

- The majority of children living with one parent lived with their single mother. About 14 percent of children living with one parent lived with their single father.[1]

- Some single parents had cohabiting partners. Twenty-six percent of children living with single fathers and 11 percent of children living with single mothers also lived with their parent's cohabiting partner. Out of all children ages 0–17, about 5.6 million (8 percent) lived with a parent or parents who were cohabiting.[1]

So where does this leave us? It leaves us with a Rube Goldberg societal conundrum that will never be unraveled even as it unfolds before our very eyes. It leaves us with:

- The overall rate of child abuse and neglect in single-parent households is 27.3 children per 1,000, whereas the overall maltreatment in two-parent households is 15.5 per 1,000.[2]

- Daughters of single parents without a father involved are 53% more likely to marry as teenagers, 711% more likely to have children as teenagers, 164% more likely to have a pre-marital birth and 92% more likely to get divorced themselves.[2]

- 90% of all homeless and runaway children are from fatherless homes—32 times the average.[2]

- 63% of youth suicides are from fatherless homes (US Dept. Of Health/Census)—5 times the average.[2]

- 85% of all children who show behavior disorders come from fatherless homes—20 times the average. (Center for Disease Control)[2]

- 80% of rapists with anger problems come from fatherless homes—14 times the average. (*Justice & Behavior*, Vol 14, p. 403-26)[2]

- 71% of all high school dropouts come from fatherless homes—9 times the average. (National Principals Association Report)[2]

These are but a few of the postgame stats. I encourage you to see the rest of the strikeout data at http://thefatherlessgeneration. wordpress.com/statistics/.[2]

These US statistics represent but a fraction of the ever-increasing single-parent households globally, not to mention the multitude of societal problems that have arisen as a result of the deterioration of the traditional family unit. Yes, thanks to the baby boomer, the feminist, and the progressive sociologist, we, along with our children, are so much better off than we were forty to fifty years ago.

The bottom line is that we adults simply don't know how to behave anymore. All our decisions and actions revolve around "me" and what makes "me" happy. We don't have a clue how to treat our spouse. We don't have any idea of the level of lifelong responsibility we're getting into or the sacrifices that we will never make in order to make a family work. We don't know how to set good examples for others, especially our kids. In short, we have no idea how to be a role model anymore. Instead we cop out and bail as soon as the going gets tough, off to procreate with the next willing participant. And all the while the kids are watching, learning, absorbing, and emulating. They emulate reality TV, rap music, twerking, professional wrestling, MMA, Ebonics, and performance enhancing drugs. They're learning from people like Jerry Springer, the Kardashian sisters, Snooki, Marilyn Manson, Miley Cyrus, Honey Boo Boo, Snoop Dog, the artist formerly known as Prince, and Paris Hilton. (Can someone please name one talent that Paris Hilton has that would make her worthy of the fame, notoriety, and success she has achieved? Can she sing, dance, act, paint, write, tell a joke, or anything? As far as I'm concerned, and according to her own video, she can't even perform oral sex satisfactorily.) In the process, kids are learning that societal ideologies, such as rugged individualism, personal fiscal responsibility, the traditional family unit, personal integrity, and personal accountability aren't worth a shit and that the most important thing in life is what makes "me" happy!

I believe the importance of role models in a young person's life, or the lack of good, strong role models in the life of a young person, can be summed up in quotes by two very diverse role models who said the same thing, only quite differently:

When a young person, even a gifted one, grows up without proximate living examples of what she may aspire to become—whether lawyer, scientist, artist, or leader in any realm—her goal remains abstract. Such models as appear in books or on the news, however inspiring or revered, are ultimately too remote to be real, let alone influential. But a role model in the flesh provides more than inspiration; his or her very existence is confirmation of possibilities one may have every reason to doubt, saying, 'Yes, someone like me can do this.'[3]

> —Sonia Sotomayor, Associate Justice of the Supreme
> Court of the United States

Or, for a simpler translation:
"If your kid needs a role model and you ain't it, you're both fucked."[3]

> —George Carlin, Comedian, Actor, Writer/Author,
> from *Brain Droppings*

The Scarlet Letter

A sixteen-year-old girl sits at home and watches television, where all the other sixteen-year-old girls are pretty, talented, and have parents they can talk to. These Hollywood glamour girls have handsome boyfriends without pimples, luxurious material things given to them by their parents, and lust in their hearts. After watching her daily shows, she goes to school, where she does not do well academically, where she has no special talent in athletics or the arts, and where she is socially awkward. What can she do to gain recognition? What can she do to be noticed? What can she do to make everyone realize that she *is* somebody and *can* accomplish something? She can get pregnant!

Once she starts to "show," everybody will have to acknowledge that some boy found her attractive and worthy of his affection. Her parents will yell at her, but at least now they're paying attention to her. The teachers will accommodate her morning sickness, and the school will empathetically provide special classes. Public aid will provide prenatal medical services. Medicare will pay for the delivery. After she delivers, she'll be entitled to day care for her child while she continues her education, if she continues it at all. Social services will assign a social worker to help her. She'll get food stamps for herself and her child through federal programs like WIC. And she will have a baby who will depend on her and give her the adoration and affection (at least for a little while) that she has craved for so long.

And she will be able to reach out to the world around her and say, "Look at me. I accomplished something!"

The CDC reports, "In 2011, a total of 329,797 babies were born to women aged 15-19 years."[1] This is a scenario that, on average, repeats itself 903 times a day in the United States. Proponents of these statistics will say we're doing a good job concerning the whole teen pregnancy issue and that the numbers have been on the decline over the past couple decades. But when you have an epidemic that is only getting marginally better and is mutating, spreading, and infecting society as a whole, is it really getting better?

The CDC report continues:

This is a record low for US teens in this age group, a drop of 8% from 2010...While reasons for the declines are not clear, teens seem to be less sexually active, and more of those who are sexually active seem to be using birth control than in previous years... Despite these declines, substantial disparities persist in teen birth rates, and teen pregnancy and childbearing continue to carry significant social and economic costs. The US teen pregnancy, birth, sexually transmitted disease (STD), and abortion rates are substantially higher than those of other western industrialized nations.[1]

My first points of observation before I continue with the report are the phrases "reasons for the declines are not clear," "substantial disparities persist," and "rates are substantially higher than those of other western industrialized nations." If the '60s social experiment of dismantling the traditional family unit that had been intact for hundreds, if not thousands of years, was such a great idea, then why are researchers today scratching their heads trying to figure out what's going on?

The CDC report then lists some of the social and economic fallout from this epidemic:

- In 2008, teen pregnancy and childbirth accounted for nearly $11 billion per year in costs to US taxpayers for increased health care and foster care, increased incarceration rates among children of teen parents, and lost tax revenue because of lower educational attainment and income among teen mothers.[1]

- Pregnancy and birth are significant contributors to high school dropout rates among girls. Only about 50% of teen mothers receive a high school diploma by 22 years of age, verses approximately 90% of women who had not given birth during adolescence.[1]

- The children of teenage mothers are more likely to have lower school achievement and drop out of high school, have more health problems, be incarcerated at some time during adolescence, give birth as a teenager, and face unemployment as a young adult.[1]

- These effects remain for the teen mother and her child even after adjusting for those factors that increased the teenager's risk for pregnancy, such as growing up in poverty, having parents with low levels of education, growing up in a single-parent family, and having poor performance in school.[1]

My second points of observation are "nearly $11 billion per year in costs to US taxpayers," "only about 50% of teen mothers receive a high school diploma by 22 years of age," and "the children of teenage mothers are more likely to..." The list goes on! I get the impression that few people realize the true extent and overall fallout of teen pregnancy. We hear a statistic here, a fact there, but how many of us truly understand the whole picture in terms of fiscal liability, emotional turmoil, and the impact on future generations. And if we are establishing the standards of conduct in this regard, then what are the chances that future generations will make corrections instead of exasperating these dilemmas even further?

Another CDC article, titled "Sexual Risk Behavior: HIV, STD, & Teen Pregnancy Prevention," presents more wonderful news concerning teen pregnancy and the "record low for US teens in this age group":

- 47.4% had (ever) had sexual intercourse[2]

- 33.7% had had sexual intercourse during the previous 3 months, and, of these

  - 39.8% did not use a condom the last time they had sex[2]

  - 76.7% did not use birth control pills or Depo-Provera to prevent pregnancy the last time they had sex[2]

- 15.3% had had sex with four or more people during their life[2]

- An estimated 8,300 young people aged 13-24 years in the 40 states reporting to CDC had HIV infection in 2009[2]

- Nearly half of the 19 million new STDs each year are among young people aged 15-24 years[2]

My third points of observation are the phrases, "47.4% had ever had sexual intercourse," "estimated 8,300 young people aged 13-24 years in the 40 states reporting to CDC had HIV infections," and "nearly half of the 19 million new STDs each year are among young people aged 15-24 years."

Someone please explain the upside of this "record low for US teens in this age group." Someone explain why all reported cases of chlamydia and gonorrhea rose in 2011, and syphilis (primary and secondary) remained unchanged from 2010.[3] A 2011 CDC Fact sheet states:

> Many cases of chlamydia, gonorrhea, and syphilis continue to go undiagnosed and unreported, and data on several additional STDs—such as human papillomavirus, herpes simplex virus, and trichomoniasis—are not routinely reported to CDC. As a result, the annual surveillance report captures only a fraction of the true burden of STDs in America. However, it provides important insights into the scope and trends of this hidden epidemic.[3]

My fourth points of observation are "continue to go undiagnosed and unreported" and "the annual surveillance report captures only a fraction of the true burden of STDs in America."

Even the CDC calls it a "hidden epidemic," although I'm confused why they refer to it as such because there's nothing "hidden" about it. We all know that the overall fallout is substantial, and it is only getting worse. Many of us may not know the exact numbers or percentages, as I just illustrated, but anyone who is halfway conscientious, responsible, and awake can take a good look around and see what's happening. When you look at the whole picture, this societal STD is not going away, but rather is a nightmare that will never end.

And so the sixteen-year-old girl sits at home and watches television, where all the other sixteen-year-old girls are living exciting and exploited lives. She watches *16 and Pregnant* to see if Josh will empathetically give up bull riding now that Mackenzie has had to retire from cheerleading. She turns the channel to *Teen Mom*, wondering what the media buzz is on Farrah's real-life porn movie she was able to make with the help of her Hollywood fame and notoriety. Her curiosity is killing her about the latest online Twitter war being waged between Alexandria and Jenelle from *Teen Mom 2* and *3*. Is Jenelle out of jail yet? She watches *The Secret Life*, wondering, with bated breath, if Adrian has been successful in seducing Ben into getting her pregnant again because Adrian knows that Ben wants to bail out of the relationship now that she has had the miscarriage. Watching *The Hard Times of R. J. Berger*, she can't help but wonder, "How big *is* R. J.'s penis?" In the show *Skins*, she ponders, "What *will* Chris do with his erection and the one thousand dollars his mom left him for the weekend?" And let's not forget to check out *Jersey Shore* to see which lucky boy will impregnate Snooki after a long night of partying and binge drinking.

Some of you may be asking yourselves, "How much worse can it get?" Some of you are thinking, "What's the big deal?" One of the great debates going on today is whether this type of media encourages teenage girls to get pregnant by the glamorization and popularization of these shows. If you don't think kids (and adults, for that matter) are influenced by what they watch on TV and what they see in the movies or in video games, then you're asleep at the wheel and a major contributor to the demise of our species. It boggles my mind that we're even debating whether these media outlets have an impact on our children. Apparently this debate has escalated to the point that *OK! Magazine* (as well as numerous other publications) is feeling the heat and needs to address the matter by stating, "Take a look at all the shows that have covered teen pregnancy in some way and tell us which one of these moments was your favorite. BTW, we're not saying that teen pregnancy is cool, we're just saying that it happens, in real life and not in real life. Wanted to clear that up."[4] Thank you *so* much, *OK! Magazine*, for clearing that up and informing us with your little disclaimer that you and the shows you advocate in no way have any impact on the choices young people make. After all, it just happens, right? By the way, how are sales going?

The stories, scenarios, and dilemmas that the impressionable youth of this world find themselves in are spiraling out of control. And if you don't think it's all that bad, I will leave you with a head-line of just one of the progressing societal nightmares from which we may never recover:

"I Am Pregnant With My Dad's Baby and We are Madly In Love With Each Other."[5] And if that doesn't warm your heart, the article continues, "But we have agreed that if my three-month scan shows a birth defect, we will terminate the pregnancy."

The epitome of the "ME" generation!

We Are All Adam Lanza's Mother

On May 18, 1927, the deadliest attack at a school in American history took place in Bath Township, Michigan, when Andrew Kehoe blew up the Bath Consolidated School killing 38 children and 6 adults, before blowing himself up.[1] The next significant school attack took place thirty-nine years later on August 1, 1966, at the University of Texas, when Charles Whitman ascended to the observation deck of the main administration building and began indiscriminately shooting innocent victims who walked the school grounds, killing fourteen and wounding thirty-one others before being killed himself.[2]

In the thirty-nine years between the Bath Consolidated School bombing in 1927 and the University of Texas slaughter in 1966, there were a total of forty-one shooting incidents in American schools, which resulted in approximately thirty-six fatalities.[3] (I say approximate fatalities because there are a number of ways one could calculate the statistic in relation to the crime. For instance, do you include people that the perpetrator killed at home or off-campus before they headed off to the school to perform their heinous deeds? Do you include the perpetrator in the statistics if he or she was killed or committed suicide during the incident? What about those who only committed suicide, but didn't harm anyone else? What about accidental shootings? What about the Kent State massacre and "Four Dead in O-HI-O"? Do they get included in the stats? In my stats, I have decided to only include the victims who were killed on or near school property at the time of the incident. However, because many of the incidents were quite unique, there were a number of gray areas to consider. If you do your own research and your numbers come out slightly different, you'll know why.)

Forty-one school shooting incidents resulting in thirty-six fatalities in thirty-nine years averages out to 1.05 school shooting incidents per year and 0.92 fatalities per year. Out of the forty-one total incidents during this thirty-nine year period, only one involved five fatalities. The other forty incidents each claimed two lives or less. These were murders or murders coupled with suicides, crimes of passion or revenge directed toward a specific individual.[3]

Fast forward another thirty-three years to April 20, 1999. On that day, eighteen-year-old Eric Harris and seventeen-year-old Dylan Klebold methodically gunned down twelve fellow students, one teacher, and wounded twenty-one others before they both committed suicide at Columbine High School in Colorado.

During the thirty-three years between the University of Texas massacre and Columbine, there were a total of eighty-one school shooting incidents, resulting in 113 fatalities.[3] This is roughly the same span of time as between the Bath massacre and the University of Texas incident (thirty-three years versus thirty-six years). During that time span, the average number of school shooting incidents per year increased from 1.05 per year on average to 2.45. In addition, the average number of annual fatalities increased from 0.92 to 3.42.

Then came Columbine. Columbine is what I like to refer to as the beginning of the modern age of "Mindless Indiscriminate School Slaughter" (MISS). It was a turning point, a shift, from people primarily killing specific people for a specific reason to adults and kids indiscriminately blowing away teachers and other kids for reasons that leave the rest of society scratching their heads, asking, "What the fuck is going on?"

From Columbine in April, 1999, until the date of this writing (August, 2013), a time span of fourteen years (less than half the time period of Bath to University of Texas or University of Texas to Columbine), there have been eighty school shooting incidents, which translates to an average of 5.71 per year, and 142 fatalities, an average of 10.14 per year.[3] These statistics represent a 133 percent increase of incidents and a 196 percent increase in fatalities for a time period of less than half the previous time period examined (fourteen years versus thirty-three years).

The above statistics only deal with school shootings and do not address the growing number of mass homicides and crimes against children outside the school arena, such as the Aurora, Colorado, movie theater shooting, which killed twelve. Furthermore, the United States by no means has a monopoly on this type of behavior. Two massacres of recent memory are the July 2011 massacre of sixty-nine people, mostly teenagers, gunned down by Andres Breivik at a youth summer camp near Oslo, Norway, and the Beslan School hostage crisis in the Russian Republic of North Ossetia, where 334 people, including 186 children, were killed in September 2004. Throw in a few genocides here and there, like Rwanda and Darfur, just to name a couple, and you can add millions of innocent victims to the list.

Unfortunately, the great debate here in the United States on how to handle these growing crises has been resurrected after the Sandy Hook tragedy in Newtown, Connecticut, where Adam Lanza went on a shooting spree that claimed the lives of six adults and twenty children. In the days and weeks following the Sandy Hook tragedy, the media, politicians, blogs, tweets, and posts were engrossed in a great finger-pointing debate, which placed the blame squarely on the shoulders of gun rights versus mental health. This is all I heard for months following the massacre: "We need to ban all guns from society" or "No, it's a mental health issue that's not being addressed."

I believe the problem is not a two-piece puzzle as the media and our leaders would have us believe, but a one-hundred-piece jigsaw puzzle. It's a fraying of society that no one really wants to fix because it would involve giving up the Mercedes and having one parent stay home to mentor and supervise the kids. It would require providing a solid and stable home environment for kids to relearn the basics of good manners and a superior work ethic—that they should get a higher education and work very hard for what they want in life and save the entitlements for those who truly need them. It would require spending much more time with the kids and, by our own example, giving them superior role models to emulate. It would require teaching them, by example, a healthy respect for their bodies—you are what you eat and everything in moderation. It would require taking away their smartphones for an hour or two at adult functions and force them to act like adults and attempt to engage in intelligent conversations with the previous generation. It would require busting their self-esteem bubble just a bit to make them realize what a dog-eat-dog world it is out there and give them some spine to deal with it. It would require teaching them, again by example, that worthwhile and meaningful relationships require hard work and commitment, and you don't just give up every time things get tough. It would involve re-teaching our children what's important in life—pop culture or culture, lifestyle or life.

Those are just a few pieces of the one-hundred-piece puzzle, and every decade since the 1960s, four or five more pieces of the societal puzzle are removed. As we look back at the puzzle, at society, so many pieces are missing that we can't tell what the picture is anymore. Thirty or forty pieces out of one hundred are missing, and we believe that putting one of two pieces back (gun ownership or mental health) is really going to make a significant difference.

So how are we going to address it? Well in the early '90s, we put the first metal detectors in schools in a futile attempt to screen out guns and knives. In some schools, kids are patted down or screened with security wands as they enter to begin their day of learning. There has been a steady increase in locker searches as well as drug and weapons searches, sometimes with canines on the scene. Cameras are installed everywhere, inside and out, to record the carnage. We have even taken away silverware in the cafeteria of many schools. It's no wonder kids don't have basic table manners anymore as they gnaw their way through their pepper steak.

Now the answers seem to be getting even more convoluted. Instead of dealing with the root cause of the epidemic, we are creating a whole new industry that I like to call the "Real Life Annihilation Children's Video Game Industry." Companies are now manufacturing smaller (approximately 2' x 3') bulletproof dry-erase boards that can be easily detached from the wall, strapped to your arm, and used like the shield of a Roman gladiator. Manufacturers are now making bulletproof backpacks for kids. (I can't wait for Justin Bieber to have his own designer line.) Of course, the kids will still have to go through the metal detectors as they are greeted by the principal at the beginning of their school day to scan those suspicious-looking backpacks. How long will it be before we outfit the kids with designer bulletproof vests? (Justin, I want royalties on that one!) Or require them to wear flip-flops to school to avoid concealing a WMD.

Is this really where we want to go? Whether you think yes or no, it *is* where we are going. We don't want to admit that we have been kicking the can down the road for decades, and the farther the can gets, the more convoluted the solution becomes, until it gets to the point where we are incapable of fixing it. If we would have addressed the problem twenty, thirty, or forty years ago with a firm hand and tough decisions, perhaps it would have been as black and white as the difference between two different choices. But now the problem is compounded by a big mix of different societal concerns that have rooted themselves so deeply into our culture that we will never get out of the weeds and eventually the jungle will take over again.

In the examples I just gave, I mentioned numerous times that we need to teach our children "by example." There lies the problem. We aren't teaching by example anymore, and if we do, it's a self-centered, convoluted example to make ourselves feel good or to wiggle our way out of a responsibility that we don't have time for. If you go back to the chapter "Whatcha Gonna Do When They Come for You?" concerning child abuse and read how adults and parents are mistreating and killing kids, as well as, how that behavior is becoming common in today's society, then why are we so shocked to see more and more kids killing kids?

We have all become too comfortable and unwilling to give up our cozy lifestyles for the sake of life. We are all addicted to the artificial pop culture we have created. We are all willing participants in the great sociological decline of our time. We are all in denial of the *real* changes that need to take place in an effort to save the sinking ship. We are all poisoned by the blissful world we have created for ourselves. We are all Adam Lanza's mother!

Welcome to the jungle!

Section 3:

Planet of the Apes

The Sounds of Silence

So now we're adults! We have survived puberty and made it to young adulthood. And what have we brought to the table? What do we bring to our society and our culture? No social skills. Our shit doesn't stink. We won't take advice from our elders because we know better, and we have all the answers. We can't deal with rejection or bullying of any kind. We always justify our actions, regardless. We come from splintered and broken homes with little or no supervision. We have no true role models to emulate and help mold us. The ones we do have are pretentious movie stars, juiced up athletes, and bitch-bangin', cop-killin' rap artists. We begin to model our own lives after that of our upbringing. We have trouble in relationships because we don't know what love is, and we don't know how to communicate with each other. We develop artificial relationships based on materialism. We have kids out of wedlock while we're still kids ourselves, and if we do get married, it isn't for long. We irresponsibly start families without any financial basis to do so. We have no realistic expectations about our future because from a very young age, we have been sheltered from all things negative and taught that our lives will be blissful and perfect. And now it's time to cut the apron strings and march headlong, not into the perfect world of our childhood dreams, but into the cruel new world that it often is.

So kick back, pop a Prozac or any one of your favorite antidepressants, and enjoy the truth about who we are and what we are becoming! Does anybody remember the truth?

And in the naked light I saw
Ten thousand people, maybe more,
People talking without speaking,
People hearing without listening,
People writing songs that voices never share,
And no one dared
Disturb the sounds of silence.

—Paul Simon

Bumper Sticker Therapy

"**W**hat could be so wrong with the innocence of bumper stickers," you may ask yourself. Well, have a seat on the tailgate of your F-150, and let me tell ya!

Back in the '60s and beyond (earlier in time), you didn't see too many bumper stickers on cars, certainly not like you do today. You didn't see them because a man's automobile was a thing to be cherished, and not meant to be a moving billboard. It was a status symbol of his hard work and contribution to society, and he waxed her and changed her oil often. (Yes, cars, like ships and planes and anything else of mechanical significance, were feminine, with no hyphenated names or transgender issues, just "she.") She was a work of art lovingly designed and built with care from Detroit, prior to the Japanese car invasion of the '70s. And if you did see an occasional bumper sticker on a car, it was a poignant expression of one's strongest convictions, like a campaign slogan for your favorite political candidate ("I Like Ike"). It could also have been a political or human rights slogan stating your support or disdain for whatever current conflict we were engaged in at the time ("Make Love Not War"). Or maybe it was simpler than that and just a sticker to support your passion for surfing (On Water, Not on the Internet) or a place you visited on your summer vacation—Grand Canyon, Key West, Disneyland.

By contrast, today's vehicles are nothing more than Facebook on wheels—way too much personal information about yourself and your precious, pretentious family that no one else cares about. And it all started in the '80s with the "Baby on Board" caution signs hanging in the rear window, causing yet another blind spot for those of us carrying children. I kept waiting for someone to back up over the neighbor's kid's bicycle, or worse yet, the kid himself, because he or she couldn't see the child as a result of the sign. It would be different if those "Baby on Board" signs actually did something, getting others to drive more cautiously and defensively around cars carrying little ones, as I'm sure was the original intent. But it didn't. It was just a "Hey, look at me!" statement. If anything, it provoked the occasional asshole into tailgating even closer just for the hell of it. It also drew the attention of the hometown pedophile when a mom left the little one in the car seat on a lovely August afternoon in Tucson, Arizona, to run into Walmart for a cold six-pack. If we have to make laws to curtail people from texting while driving or drinking and driving, then a "Baby on Board" sign isn't going to do shit!

Modern-day vehicle owners ride around with bumper stickers in the shape of a bone that says, "I [heart] my Schnauzer." That's cool. I love my Schnauzer too. The only difference is I don't feel the need to incessantly broadcast it to every stranger who tailgates me with their high beams on. It's more of a private, interpersonal canine relationship between the bitch and I. You would be doing society a blessing if you just picked up their crap when they shit on people's lawns instead of professing your undying love for them on your car bumper.

Or how about all the "My Little Precious Darling is an Honor Roll Student at Such–and–Such Elementary School" bumper stickers? That's great that your precious darling is an honor roll student. Seriously it is! Apparently it's become such a rarity that those of us who have custody of these young ones on weekends are just ecstatic about it and can't wait to profess it to unsuspecting total strangers passing on the right because we don't know what the left lane is for. Why don't you just take little Jonny out for ice cream at Chuck E. Cheese for making the honor roll? I'm sure he would appreciate that much greater than a bumper sticker. And besides, the jury is still out on whether or not little Jonny is going to be the next representative from your congressional district or a brilliant research scientist who discovers a cure for stupidity. You never see those bumper stickers, do you? "My Son Graduated Sigma Cum Laude with a PhD in Physics." Now there's a bumper sticker worth bragging about!

I guess we do see stickers like "My Daughter is in the Army," and that's cool because at least it's something that someone actually accomplished and is worthy of notoriety. Not to mention the fact that they are putting their lives on the line so that the rest of us can do our nine-to-five jobs, come home, kick our feet up, watch hours of reality TV, spew every uneducated opinion we have about every political issue there is even though we didn't even vote, and then protest at their funerals—the modern-day equivalent of spitting on them.

Or what about the little stick figures on everybody's rear window that shows a mommy, a daddy, two kids, a dog, and a cat? Who cares! Why is there a need to tell everyone driving behind you who and what consists of your family! I don't care if you have two cats and one dog. I don't care if you have two dogs and one cat. I don't care if you have two girls, or a boy and a girl, or a boy and one transgender girl. I don't know you, and I don't care!

I have, for many years, lived by a self-imposed principle that I will not date a woman who has an "I [Heart] My Cat" bumper sticker on the back of her car. To me, "I [Heart] My Cat" translates to "Hi, nice to meet you. My name is Insecure Needy

High-Maintenance. What's yours"? (I even got the hyphenated last name in there.) I guess that's one of those times where we can be blessed that the unsuspecting gal is unknowingly broadcasting her insecurities to the world. Thank you for saving us the cost of dinner and a movie!

It's great that you love your wife, your kid, and your family pet. But do us a favor and keep it to yourself, Mr. Me Generation, because no one else really cares. Take the, "I [Heart] my Wife" bumper sticker down and grow a pair because the only thing it says about you is that you are at the bottom of the Homo sapien food chain. And I'm glad your eight-year-old is an honor roll student, but *I'm* not going to buy him an ice cream cone for fear of being investigated as a child molester. Just keep it in the family, will ya? Yes, bumper stickers of today are just a way to cover up the fact that we never made it out of the middle-class, so we advertise to the world personal things to make us feel better about ourselves and get bragging rights on points that no one else really cares about.

You may be wondering why I am wasting a chapter on something as mundane and insignificant as bumper stickers. I wanted to get section three started off on a light note. Since this section delves into the decline of society as a whole, I didn't want to start off too heavy before you had ample time to feel the effects from your Prozac. I wanted to start off slow, yet point out just one of the hundreds upon hundreds of incidental and seemingly harmless ways we have become a self-absorbed society that really cares about very little other than "me."

> Beam me up Scotty!
> There's No Intelligent Life Down Here!

May I Help You Pretty Please?

*I*n the 1930s through the 1960s (Actually from the '60s back to the Stone Age), no one had to be taught customer service skills. No one had to be schooled in how to speak to a customer, how to act in front of a customer, or how to engage a customer. People just did it, even young people. They did it because it was taught to them at home, and it was reflected in the environment in which they lived. Oh, sure, shopgirls and other professions alike were trained in etiquette specific to their job, but it was an easy task because all of the foundational basics were already there. Young people were brought up to be courteous and kind to people and to have respect for their elders. So when they got old enough to go out and get their first jobs, no one had to teach them those skills because they weren't skills. It was simply common sense that was ingrained or the influence of their upbringing, and probably a combination of both.

Today, having good or even marginal customer service is a "skill." Corporations spend a vast amount of resources sending employees to classes to learn these skills that only became classified as such over the last forty to fifty years when they began to disappear from society. Nowadays if you have superior customer service, it's because you took a class and you have a framed certificate hanging in your cubicle to prove it.

Most of us experience poor customer service routinely as we go through our daily lives. Just the other day I was ordering at a fast-food restaurant. The cashier said, "May I take your order?" As I began to order, another employee was talking to one of her coworkers over by the drive-thru window. She was going off in a louder-than-necessary voice about another employee who worked there: "She don't do nothin. I have to clean up after her crap all the time." I could not see the woman, but could clearly hear her as she was standing only ten to fifteen feet away.

The woman taking my order looked in her direction and said in a managerial tone, "I have a customer up front."

The disgruntled employee replied, "I'm back here. They're up there." (I'm not even sure what she meant by that.)

"I can still hear you," I fired back. There was no reply from the mysterious voice by the window, but the woman taking my order looked at me; she was very embarrassed and profusely apologized. Obviously she had a certificate hanging in her cubicle somewhere.

I can't tell you how many times I have been in this very same situation over the past year, placing my order at the counter and in the middle of ordering, the cashier is interrupted by another customer wanting a refill or by a coworker asking them a question. The cashier abruptly disengages from me, speaks to the other individual, and then turns her attention back to me as if nothing happened, at which time I am usually asked to repeat what I just said. "Yes, this is 'to go,' for the third time," I would reply. Or how about when you're at the drive-thru, and the person is handing you your order, looking right at you, but he or she is talking on the headset to the person in the car behind yours. You think the employee is talking to you, so you answer them back in some whimsical, confused voice until you realize it's not you that he or she is talking to. Then you feel like an idiot. And why is it that more often than not, you pull away from the drive-thru window only to discover that they gave you a straw but no napkins. Then there's the overly friendly cashier who you've never met before, but she apparently thinks you're her therapist because, out of nowhere, she starts spewing way too much information about her boyfriend and his ex-girlfriend, when all you're trying to do is pay for your Happy Meal. Most of these customer service faux pas are so incidental and common that we hardly seem to notice anymore. It's expected and the norm.

Enough griping about the fast-food industry, as they by no means have a monopoly on poor customer service. We all complain about the ten prompts we have to go through to speak with a real live Homo sapien over the phone, if we can prompt our way to a real person at all. Or having to take your car back because it wasn't repaired correctly, then having to deal with a bunch of BS from the car repair shop because they don't want to be bothered or spend the money to fix it correctly or to your satisfaction. Then there are the times when you're in a grocery store or a big warehouse operation like Lowe's or Costco, and you ask an employee where something is, and they say, "I think it's on aisle sixteen." You *think* it's on aisle sixteen? What this really means is that you don't really know, do you? You're taking your best guess and sending me on some wild goose chase over to aisle sixteen so that another customer service representative on aisle sixteen can tell me that they *think* it's on aisle two. I have a brilliant customer service idea for the suggestion box. Why don't you take me by the hand and *show* me where it is? Walmart used to be the only operation I know of that went out of their way to actually show customers where stuff was, but even they have gotten slack in this regard over the years.

There are probably a number of contributing factors for this decline of manners and customer service in society, but I would like to zero in on two primary suspects. In the '70s, if you wanted to get a business letter to someone, you scratched it out on a legal pad, got your secretary to type it with this thing called a typewriter and a carbon copy, or you made a copy of it in the copy machine when you were done. Then you had to have the courier drive it across town or you stuck it in the mail, and the recipient got it the next day if you were lucky and the post office was on the ball. Today your secretary can type up the letter on a computer with the benefit of backspace and cut-and-paste, forward it to you as an attachment. You can then download it on your cell phone, proof it, and forward it to the individual all in five minutes while driving and texting in rush-hour traffic. Magic! The computer age and these conveniences of the day have allowed us to increase our productivity a hundredfold from thirty or forty years ago. The flip side of that coin is that we have created an environment where, in order to keep up with the Joneses and stay competitive, we place the emphasis on how fast and how cheap we can produce a good or service (not to be confused with how *efficiently* or how *affordably* we can produce a product or service). A perfect example is the drive-thru person who hands us our meal while talking to the person in the car behind ours. And who can blame them? If we spend more than five minutes in the drive-thru, we're complaining because we will be late clocking in from our thirty-minute lunch break and written up by our supervisor, who is in a pissy mood themselves because they didn't get a straw with their Happy Meal.

There used to be a day not too long ago when gas stations were called "service stations," and they were called that for a reason. A service station attendant would walk up to your car window, ask you if you wanted to "Fill'er up, regular or premium," and proceed to do so. While the car was filling up, the attendant would, on his own accord, clean your front and rear windshield, and then ask you if you would like for them to check under the hood, all while you sat in the cozy confines of your car listening to "Hey Jude" on your 8-track player. But those days are gone, unless of course you live in New Jersey or some other forced-gas-union-labor state where it is unlawful for you to pump your own gas. But even then, ask the gas station attendant if they could pretty please check under the hood for you, and I'm sure you'll get a look of disarray or a "not my job" retort. Speed and efficiency have taken precedence over customer service to the point where, not only is it a rarity to get good customer service, but often enough, you can't get it at all.

The second primary culprit would undoubtedly have to do with our interpersonal skills or lack thereof. Aside from the fact that a growing number of young people today are not taught basic manners or respect for others, they also don't learn basic communication skills. Just look at them (and even adults)—everywhere you go, people have their noses stuck to their cell phones, disengaged from their surroundings and environment. No one knows how to strike up a pleasant conversation with a new acquaintance or how to make intelligent "small talk" with their new boss at the coffee machine. Our speech and interaction with others has been reduced to a mumbling of abbreviations and acronyms in a text message. No one knows how to speak to people anymore, and no one cares; not to mention the fact that no one can do simple math in their heads. No cursive, no basic math abilities, no interpersonal communication, no customer service skills. Just punch the big pretty button that says "Happy Meal" and life is good.

"I'll have a number five, supersized please."

"Uh, OK, that will be, uh, seven-oh-two."

"Here's ten."

"Uh, OK. Your change is, uh, two dollars and, uh, ninety-eight cents."

"Oh, wait a minute. I have two cents."

"Um, OK, but I already rang it up."

"It's three dollars. Just give me fuckin' three dollars back!"

"Like, um, uh…"

"Can I get that 'to go' please?"

Now that's what I call putting in your two cents worth!

Take This Job and Love It

*L*ooking back on my life, there were certainly a few jobs that come to mind that I am not too proud of. Being a bag boy at my local grocery store wasn't anything to write home about, but then again, I was in high school and still living at home. Delivering pizzas to help make ends meet when I was in my early thirties was a bit depressing. I was just happy that my ten-year high school reunion had passed, and I had another seven years to go before my twenty-year reunion—plenty of time to make amends for my menial working-class status. Although I may not have been proud of these jobs, I did them out of financial necessity and to the best of my ability without complaining.

Apparently, doing your job and doing it well isn't good enough anymore. Spiritually and intellectually, we need the self-affirmation perks that go along with the job description. And who can blame us? Our entire lives have been a beautiful snow globe where we get, and have come to not only expect but also need, constant reinforcement and encouragement. One of those ever-present, self-righteous, self-gratifying perks that we have come to rely on is, sadly, the fictitious elevation of our job status so we feel better about ourselves. Any little pat on the back we can get, we'll take. We need it! We have to have it! And the next thing you know, everybody's an engineer or a consultant of some sort, a representative of this or that, or an expert technician of technically technical affairs. If people were as obsessed with the quality of work they produced as they were with their job titles, I think we would all get better cell phone reception.

Yes indeed, let's all hold our heads and our egos a little higher knowing that we are:

Housewives: Domestic Engineers

Grocery Store Stockers/Baggers: Courtesy Clerks

Paperboys: Media Distribution Personnel

Secretaries: Receptionists

Receptionists: Administrative Assistants

Caregivers: Direct Support Professionals

Janitors: Custodians

Custodians: Custodial Engineers

Garbage Men: Public Sanitation Engineers

Weathermen: Meteorologists

Bartenders: Mixologists

Prison Guards: Correctional Technicians

Security Guards: Theft Prevention Officers/Surveillance Officers

Policemen: Law Enforcement Officers

Salesmen: Customer Service Representatives

Bank Loan Officers: Customer Relationship Managers

Window Cleaners: Transparency Enhancement Facilitators

Stewardesses: Flight Attendants

Hairdressers: Stylists

Waiters/Waitresses: Servers

Food Preppers: Sandwich Artists

Lunch Ladies: Education Center Nourishment Consultants

Tour Guides: Historical Interpreters

Motel Maids: Housekeepers

Babysitters: Nannies

Nannies: Au Pairs

Illegal Aliens: Undocumented Immigrants

I'm not going to get too carried away and only pointed out some of the more common title transgressions. There are hundreds upon hundreds of these new hybrid positions now available for hire. After all, why would anyone care to be a "Lunch Lady" when they can be an "Education Center Nourishment Consultant"? Similarly, why be a "Window Cleaner" instead of a "Transparency Enhancement Facilitator"? Maybe, back when I was in my early thirties, if I could have been a "Gourmet Food Service Delivery Enhancement Facilitator in Thirty Minutes or Less Personnel" instead of a "Pizza Delivery Guy," my career path may have been quite different and better, I'm sure. (I can already see the intellectual gears turning in the food service industry over that new title.) I wonder how many of those people would rather keep their fictitious, elevated title than the pay raise they never got to coincide with their new title.

And, of course, it didn't stop there, as every profession has to have its day in the sun to complement its elevated status. I have sympathy for some seemingly mundane days of recognition, such as National Secretaries Day. (The creators of this day really need to get up with the times and update the name to Administrative Assistants Day.) Secretaries are often abused and unappreciated by their bosses even though they're the ones who typically put up with all the bosses' crap and make them look good day in and day out. I have oftentimes seen secretaries spend more money on their bosses and treat them nicer on National Bosses Day than I have seen the bosses treat their secretaries on National Secretaries Day.

But of course, it wouldn't be fair for some to have a day and not others, so now everyone has their day: National Medical Librarian Month (not to be confused with your standard librarian month), National Records & Information Management Month, National Custodial Workers Day, National Physical Therapy Month, National Weatherpersons Day, National Provider Appreciation

Day, National Waitstaff Day, National Medical Science Liaison Awareness & Appreciation Day.[1]

I guess having the first Monday in September designated as Labor Day just wasn't good enough. And who decides whether you get a day, a week, or a month of recognition? If I were a weatherperson who got his or her annual day in the sun, I would be royally pissed that medical librarians get a month. It used to be that every dog had its day, but now every human being has their day, week, or month!

Earlier in this book, I referenced JFK's famous line, "Ask not what your country can do for you. Ask what you can do for your country." No one cares about that anymore. Many don't even know what it means or what it is in reference too. The only thing people care about today is "me." "What's in it for me?" is the mantra of the times: "When am I going to get *my* raise?" "When am I going to get *my* promotion?" "That's not *my* problem!" I think that the main purpose of the modern-day job description is so that people can sit around and assert, "That's not *my* job."

On October 26, 1967, six months before he was assassinated, Martin Luther King Jr. spoke to a group of students at Barratt Junior High School in Philadelphia. That short but sweet speech has often been referred to as the "street sweeper speech." It reads, in part:

> If it falls your lot to be a street sweeper, sweep streets like Michelangelo painted pictures, sweep streets like Beethoven composed music, sweep streets like Leontyne Price sings before the Metropolitan Opera. Sweep streets like Shakespeare wrote poetry. Sweep streets so well that all the hosts of heaven and earth will have to pause and say: Here lived a great street sweeper who swept his job well.[2]

Where have all the good street sweepers gone?

Sign, Sign, Everywhere's a Sign!

Do This, Don't Do That, Can't You Read The Sign?

S ince when did mothers stop teaching their kids how to wash their hands? Does anybody "wash up" before supper anymore? I don't remember when it was exactly, probably around the early to mid-nineties I'm guessing, but I do remember *where* I was. I had just finished using the restroom in an elegant restaurant and turned to the towel dispenser to dry my hands before returning to sit with my guests. As I ripped the towel from the dispenser, there it was, staring me right in the face: "All Employees *Must* Wash Hands Before Returning To Work." I stood there, wiping my hands, staring at the sign, and a strange feeling of confusion and discomfort came over me. It was just odd.

Why is this sign here? I thought to myself. *Is it really necessary? Does this fine establishment have hygiene issues?* I began to wonder if I should ask to see their health permit or their sanitation score. I began to wonder what the interesting but unusual taste in my beef stroganoff might have been. I began to wonder if I should cancel dessert! When I returned to the table, I began to stare at the waiter's hands when he asked if anyone needed more coffee.

"No, thanks. I'm good. No, really." I replied, placing my hand over my coffee cup.

Today that same elegant restaurant is still there, and it still has that same sign posted, with an addition of an even more disturbing sign right next to it—a lovely laminated, full-color, 11" x 8 1/2" sign that has step-by-step instructions (six steps in all, accompanied by illustrations) on the proper way to wash your hands. Do we really need signs to tell us *how* to wash our hands? Apparently so, because these two signs have become commonplace in every aspect of our society: restaurants, office buildings, municipal buildings, gas stations, grocery stores, assembly buildings, and almost everywhere except, perhaps, in the privacy of our own homes. Maybe if we hung them up behind the toilets in our homes, then perhaps we could take them down everywhere else.

One lovely day in February 1992, Stella Liebeck pulled up to the drive-thru at her favorite McDonald's in Albuquerque, New Mexico, ordered a coffee, got the coffee at the window, put it between her knees, pulled the lid off to add creamer, and spilled it all over her crotch, causing third-degree burns. A jury of twelve Homo ignoramuses awarded her a judgment in excess of two million dollars. This case has become infamous in the legal world and spurred much heated debate over tort reform.

Supporters of Stella will tell you it was a great victory over greedy, insanely rich corporate America. They'd go on to say Stella was originally seeking compensation of a measly twenty grand, but stubborn McDonald's said no, so, in the end, McDonald's got what it had coming! My question is, "When does personal accountability come into the picture?" Apparently it doesn't. I could rationalize this lawsuit if the lid had popped off while the drive-thru "Customer Service Barista Engineer (aka minimum wage working, pimple-faced, hormonal teen job title wannabe) was handing the coffee to Stella or if the lid was improperly secured to the cup and randomly popped off while Stella was taking a sip. But it didn't. Stella placed the cup between her own legs and pulled the lid off to add creamer, spilling coffee on herself in the confines of her own vehicle. You can argue (as the defense attorneys did) that the coffee was served too hot, but if you research what the National Coffee Association recommends as an appropriate temperature or what temperature Starbucks serves its coffee, you will find the temperature of Stella's coffee was certainly within reason.[1] Not only that, but can you imagine what the unintended consequences would have been had McDonald's gone ahead and paid Stella the twenty thousand dollars she was originally seeking? Every scumbag in town would be ordering drive-thru coffee, only to claim a faulty lid caused a second-degree burn on their knee!

As the years passed, more and more Homo sapiens jumped on the "Hey, I can screw rich corporate America and get rich too" bandwagon, and there was no shortage of lawyers standing in line eager to exploit the system and no shortage of Homo ignoramus juries to complete the process. As a result, we now have signs and warning labels on everything and anything, reminding us not to be stupid and use a little common sense because apparently there is no personal integrity or accountability for anything anymore.

Here are just a few of the thousands upon thousands of warning labels on common household and commercial products that I found on the website RinkWorks.com (www.rinkworks.com):[2]

"For external use only!"—On a curling iron

"Do not use while sleeping."—On a hair dryer

"Recycled flush water unsafe for drinking."—On a toilet at a public sports facility in Ann Arbor, Michigan

"This product not intended for use as a dental drill."—On an electric rotary tool

"Do not drive with sunshield in place."—On a cardboard sunshade that keeps the sun off the dashboard

"Do not use near fire, flame, or sparks."—On an "Aim-n-Flame" fireplace lighter

"Do not eat toner."—On a toner cartridge for a laser printer

"May irritate eyes."—On a can of self-defense pepper spray

"Caution: contents hot!"—On a Domino's Pizza box

"Caution: hot beverages are hot!"—On a coffee cup

"Do not use orally."—On a toilet bowl cleaning brush

"Please keep out of reach of children."—On a butcher knife

"Do not use for drying pets."—In the manual for a microwave oven

"For use on animals only."—On an electric cattle prod

"Warning: knives are sharp!"—On the packaging of a sharpening stone

"Warning: has been found to cause cancer in laboratory mice."—On a box of rat poison

"Caution: remove infant before folding for storage."—On a portable stroller

"Do not iron clothes on body."—On packaging for a Rowenta iron

"Wearing of this garment does not enable you to fly."—On a child-sized Superman costume

"Warning: do not use if you have prostate problems."—On a box of Midol PMS relief tablets

"Not for human consumption."—On a package of dice

"Warning: May contain nuts."—On a package of peanuts

"Do not use orally after using rectally."—In the instructions for an electric thermometer

Now that most of you are laughing your ass off, let me bring you back to reality by reminding you that none of these warning labels would ever have been put on any of these products had someone not killed or maimed someone or something by doing exactly what the warning label warned against. No manufacturer or individual with a smidgen of common sense would ever conceive of the notion that anyone would try to dry Fido in the microwave, that someone would actually drive off in their car with the sunshade still on the windshield, that a lighter could actually

start a fire, or that someone with a peanut allergy might not realize that a can of peanuts actually contains peanuts. Yes, we have
the Darwin awards, attorneys, and juries filled with intellectually
impaired apes to thank for this monumental intellectual decline
into the abyss of stupidity. I actually know someone who burned
herself while trying to iron a small wrinkle out of her blouse while
she was wearing it (Don't worry, Sandy, I keep my sources con-
fidential). Had the warning label not been on the iron, I'm sure
Sandy would be a multimillionaire by now.

They say that in the future, everyone will have a barcode tattoo
to identify who they are. I believe that, but I also believe that right
next to the barcode there should be a warning label that reads:

WARNING:
**Homo sapiens are a hazard to themselves. Lack of common
sense can cause people to do really, really stupid things that
can result in serious injury or death. If you are unsure of
your ability to think rationally, by all means, don't do anything about it and seek legal counsel at once.
Live life at your own risk!**

Super Morbidly Obese

After last week, I can't go to my favorite Asian buffet any-more. Not for lunch, not for dinner, not for nothing. It's not because the tuna wasn't sushi grade, and I got sick as a dog. It's not because I abused the privilege of the unwritten all-you-can-eat rule by going to the buffet bar ten to fifteen times, returning to my seat with mounds of food on my plate, egg foo young noodles hang-ing off the sides, and miniature balls of sticky rice rolling onto the floor, only to leave a third of the food on my plate for the Chinese server, Jodi, to haul it away to the dumpster. No, it's not about that at all. It was a self-imposed exile that will keep me away until the effects of professional therapy give me the courage to go back again. And it was all because of an oversight on my behalf: I did not bring a book or magazine along to read as I usually do when dining out by myself, and I was forced to watch people.

Gazing across the dining room was like looking at an optical illusion where you don't see it at first, but as you keep staring at it, the pieces start to come together and suddenly there it is—some-thing completely different than what you perceived moments ago. By default of observation, my favorite Asian restaurant had become an origami nightmare. There was one, then another, then another, then another—yes, four motorized scooters busily buzzing about. Two of the four occupants of these scooters were equipped with an oxygen tube hooked from ear-to-ear, passing under their hairy nostrils, and connected to a tank clumsily attached to the scooter seat. And although all four individuals were morbidly obese, with a good portion of their cheeks hanging off both sides of their miraculous motorized devices, all had the coordination and dexterity to balance an overly full plate of food in one hand while navigating their scooter back to their handicap accessible table with their other hand without hitting anything or spilling a drop—a feat soon to be revered and studied by David Blaine, I'm sure. Not to mention the people with canes, walkers, or with a wobble in their walk that required them to shift their entire body weight directly over their alternating hip, each futile step like some kind of zombie dance move from Michael Jackson's "Thriller!"

Forty years ago, being obese was something to be frowned upon. But then as we slowly let it creep into our children's lives, it was no longer so bad and became normal. And once it became normal, of course we had to push the envelope a little further and create another category of "morbidly obese," defined by the CDC as someone who has a "BMI (Body Mass Index) greater than or equal to 40 kilos per meter squared."[1] If you can't figure that calculation out, the article continues by saying, "Among Americans 20 years or older, 28% are obese and 5% are morbidly obese." That means, on average, 5.6 out of every twenty American adults are fat, and one out of every twenty are morbidly fat. Just the sound of that makes me shudder.

My handy-dandy, *Webster's II Dictionary* defines morbid as: **1.** Of, pertaining to, or caused by disease. **2.** Preoccupied with unwholesome feelings or matters. **3.** Gruesome: grisly.

If the name isn't bad enough to scare you into being skinny, or at least losing a little weight in an effort to add a few years to your life, then I don't know what will. But of course it doesn't bother anyone because, as I mentioned earlier, despite the health and wellness trend in this country, most people will eat what they want, won't exercise, smoke, abuse their bodies, then run to the doctor for a pill when they feel like shit, and then have the nerve to bitch and complain about the high cost of hospitalization and health insurance. And why should they do anything different now that society has made obesity a "disease," and we can run to our doctor for any number of prescription drugs or procedures that the doc will be more than happy to do because he has a condo in St. Croix that he needs to pay off. Yes, come on down, ladies and gentlemen, for your gastric bypass, or a gastric band, or a gastric sleeve, accompanied by some liposuction to get you back to that twenty-five-year-old shapely figure you used to have. Oh, I'm sorry, you are twenty-five! Well, if all else fails, there's your little scooter to make it all better.

And now that morbidly obese is becoming the social norm, or socially acceptable at the very least, we humans have pushed the envelope and created a new category called "super morbidly obese." In another twenty years, when super morbidly obese becomes the acceptable norm, what will the next category be called? Allow me to speculate: 38 percent of the population will be obese, 26 percent will be morbidly obese, 18 percent will be super morbidly obese, 10 percent will be super terminally perverse on-death's-door morbidly obese (aka STPODDMO), leaving 8 percent of us in the healthy to good-old-fat range! And life will go on. We will keep adding more and more handicap parking spaces until a majority of the parking lots are full of them. Supermarkets and retail stores will supply *only* motorized carts for its customers, taking away any last holdout of exercise we might be forced to get. Bathroom stalls will be as big as a *Cribs* master bedroom walk-in closet, and the Empire State Building will be updated with an exterior handicap ramp that goes round and round from top to bottom, confusing Japanese tourists into thinking it's the Guggenheim.

Yes, ladies and gentlemen, apparently we *can* have our cake and eat it too! It's justifiable. It's a disease. It's the norm. Run to your doctor, and he will fix it so you can shove more cake down your throat! It's OK because it's your right. That's what insurance is for!

Just do it!

Doctor, Doctor, Give Me the News!

---

*H*ave a seat, Mr. Me Generation. Your test results are back, and I'm afraid I have some good news and some bad news. The bad news is that we cannot cure your stupidity. The good news is that we now have a magic pill that will relieve you of the symptoms of your reality, symptoms that began innocently enough in the early '70s during the dawn of the self-esteem movement, but have now developed into an all-out societal plague.

ODD: Oppositional Defiant Disorder

Back in the old days, we used to just spank our kids when they needed it. Between the overabundance of child abuse running amuck in this world and the progressive sociologists, we can't spank them anymore, so let's just heavily medicate them because that's so much more appropriate.

There are certainly many children out there who legitimately have anger management issues and/or chemical imbalances in their bodies that would warrant an ODD diagnosis. I have seen it in kids who, for whatever reason, have been passed around from foster home to foster home. I have seen it in kids who live with alcoholic or abusive parents. In legitimate cases, it is a tragic and difficult disorder to deal with. But I have also seen it diagnosed in kids who have never been disciplined in any meaningful way and are perfectly capable of behaving themselves with just a little bit of routine discipline and structure. A simple example of this would be when a young, modern-day couple brings their odious offspring to Grandma and Grandpa's house, or perhaps Great-grandma and Great-grandpa's house, to hang out for a week while the parents go away to celebrate their fifth wedding anniversary. The little one is accustomed to hearing "no" all day long, occasionally being put in her thinking chair for five minutes at a time, but Gramps doesn't put up with that crap. Gramps says no twice, maybe three times, then Ms. Odious gets a swat on the behind, and *Dora the Explorer* is taken away for the next hour or two. The first twenty-four hours or so are usually a living hell, but after that, Little Ms. Odious transforms into Little Miss Sunshine, and everyone lives happily ever after for the rest of the week. Once the child understands what the expectations are and what type of behavior they can and cannot get away with, they conform quite nicely. And when Mom and Dad return from a week of trying to save their marriage, back home to the same old routine, the child's behaviors are back to "normal." I have seen this happen time and time again over the years, and it is amazing how differently children will behave with a little meaningful discipline and structure in their lives.

I guess my big question is, at what point does a behavioral issue become a disorder or a disease? Because let's face it, there are plenty of parents who are incapable of disciplining their children in any meaningful way, yet they want the disruptive behavior to go away. As I mentioned in an earlier chapter, Sigmund Freud once said, "Children are completely egoistic. They feel their needs intensely and strive ruthlessly to satisfy them."[1] That being so, the longer parents let children get away with their horrendous behavior, the more the child thinks of it as normal. Oftentimes it gets worse. Hearing "no" all day long is normal. Sitting in a thinking chair for five minutes at a time is normal. And, of course, there are plenty of doctors willing and able to *treat* the little lad with prescription drugs and therapy because, after all, the doc can't bill your insurance company for discipline.

A friend of mine worked for many years as an office manager for two inner-city criminal defense attorneys. She would occasionally see parents literally drag their kids kicking and screaming into the office and meet with the attorney to see if he or she could get them disability benefits based on the fact that their child was Beelzebub. After one such incident, she told me, "If I behaved like that when I was a kid, I got my ass beat." But what was even more disturbing for her was the parents' behaviors and interactions with the children while waiting to see the attorney. A parent would often roughly yank their kid's arm, screaming at them to "Shut up!" My friend continued by saying, "In most cases, it's the parents that need their ass beat. All they're doing is taking advantage of the system and looking for an entitlement simply for being horrible parents."

And it shouldn't be too difficult in today's world to take advantage of the system and get disability benefits for your child's behavior issues. After all, even the CDC states, "It is estimated that 13-20 percent of children living in the United States (up to 1 out of 5 children) experience a mental disorder in a given year and an estimated $247 billion is spent each year on childhood mental disorders."[2] When I was a child growing up in the 1960s my behavior was normal pesky childlike behavior. Today that same behavior is a mental disorder.

So again I ask, "At what point does a behavioral issue become a disorder or a disease?" Apparently it becomes one when we can't be effective parents; when we stop trying; when we start taking the easy, medicated way out; when we start looking at it as a disease for which we are eligible for a financial entitlement handout because we can't do our jobs as parents to begin with; and when we are failing our children, our families, and our society.

SAD: Seasonal Affective Disorder

For millions and millions of years, man has endured the changing of the seasons—four yearly changes to be exact, except for the Ice Age years, when spring, summer, and fall disappeared for a while. (Perhaps with global warming, in another one hundred years or so, we will be able to eradicate seasonal affective disorder. Wouldn't that be great? Not really because it will only be replaced with nonseasonal affective disorder—people who are deeply and adversely affected by the same season, after season.) Man accepted the changing of the seasons as part of life and didn't think twice about it because that's how God created it. It was reality. And you were grateful for it. You used the winter to prepare for the harvest, and you took advantage of the summer to stock up on canned goods and firewood in preparation for a long winter.

When the seasons change from summer to fall and the weather begins to cool, it's normal for many people to feel a strange sense of lonesomeness or despair. (Why? I'm not sure because for the past three months, all I have heard is people constantly bitching and complaining about how hot it is.) I experience those same feelings of gloom. The leaves briefly turn amazing colors, and then wilt and die. The green grass turns to brown. More clouds seem to obscure the sun. The days grow shorter. Life seemingly becomes bland and barren. But you know what? That's life! And in a couple of weeks, I come to appreciate the cool nights, I begin looking forward to a little snow here and there, the gloom goes away and life is good again. And besides, there's nothing I can do about it anyway—except run to my doctor to get my magic selective serotonin reuptake inhibitor. Perhaps I'll ask for some "light therapy" to make my reality go away, or, at the very least, alter my reality into something artificial that I can deal with.

The Mayo Clinic website states:

Light therapy is a way to treat seasonal affective disorder (SAD) by exposure to artificial light. Seasonal affective disorder is a type of depression that occurs at a certain time of year, usually in the fall or winter. During light therapy, you sit or work near a device called a light therapy box. The box gives off bright light that mimics natural outdoor light. Light therapy is thought to affect brain chemicals linked to mood, erasing SAD symptoms. Using a light therapy box may also help with other types of depression, sleep disorders and other conditions. Light therapy is also known as bright light therapy or phototherapy.[3]

Light therapy sounds like a great thing for Eskimos. If I didn't know any better, I would move to northern Alaska and become an igloo-to-igloo light box salesman, but something tells me most Eskimos are perfectly fine with their reality and their eight months of winter every year. I find it really, hard to believe that instead of logging off of Facebook and turning off the reality TV, going outside, and getting a little fresh air, exercise, and sunshine every once in a while, people would rather go out and buy a special lamp that mimics sunshine to make themselves feel better. We already have the fireplace channel that shows nothing more than a fire burning in a fireplace 24-7. Perhaps we can have a sunshine channel that people can turn to when they're feeling gloomy. This is yet another perfect example of how we refuse to deal with the root cause of an issue, only to turn around and create a new industry and new products to help us cope with our dysfunctional reality.

SAD is one of the classic, quintessential examples of how pathetically we are regressing as a species. Is it really any wonder why we can't solve critical problems of the day when a growing number of us can't even deal with the changing of the seasons?

SWD: Shift Work Disorder

Are you serious? Dad used to go into work at 7:00 a.m., but the company added a second shift. Now Dad has to go in at 4:00 p.m. It disrupted his sleep cycle. It is an adjustment to his family life when he gets Jocelyn and Peter every other weekend. It's an overall pain in the ass, but dad does it because it's a good job, and he can't afford to lose it right now. And you know what? In a couple of weeks, his body adjusts, and he is back on track with his new routine. Life is good again. But the modern-day Homo sapien can't do that. The modern-day Homo sapien would rather not give it the old college try, preferring to just pop some pills to make it all go away.

The big drug being pushed these days for SWD is Nuvigil. I hear commercials all the time on the radio and TV. I can't imagine what the pharmaceutical companies marketing budget for this drug is, but I know it's huge. And I know they wouldn't be spending it if they weren't confident of a huge return on their investment. The website Nuvigil.com (www.nuvigil.com) boasts wonderful benefits, saying:

> Nuvigil may cause serious side effects, including a serious rash or a serious allergic reaction that may affect parts of your body such as your liver or blood cells, and may result in hospitalization and be life threatening...Mental (psychiatric) symptoms, including: depression, feeling anxious, sensing things that are not really there, extreme increase in activity (mania), thoughts of suicide, aggression, or other mental problems.[4]

But hey, at least you made it to work on time. It kind of sucks for the rest of us, though. I mean, here you have someone who is already overworked and underpaid. The company has, without their input, told them that they have to move to second shift or else. They're not too happy about it and have a difficult time adjusting. They start taking prescription drugs to help themselves cope. The next thing you know, they're feeling anxious, depressed, hallucinating, and have feelings of aggression or suicide. And the rest of us are standing around, dumbfounded as to why they just blew away six of their coworkers. The website goes on to say, "Common side effects of Nuvigil are headache, nausea, dizziness, and trouble sleeping." Trouble sleeping? WTF! I thought that's what this drug was supposed to…oh, never mind.

Pretty soon we'll be seeing Two Full-Time Jobs Disorder (TFTJD) or Full-Time College Student, Part-Time Job Syndrome (FTCSPTJS). In the meantime, we have Red Bull, Monster, Reload, Full Throttle, AMP Energy, Verve, Rockstar, 5-Hour Energy, and a host of other potentially unhealthy energy drinks to help us cope with our exhausting day. What happened to a good old twelve-ounce can of Coca-Cola or Mountain Dew for that after lunch, midafternoon pick-me-up? Suddenly that wasn't good enough anymore, so we made the twenty-ounce soft drink the norm. But that only lasted a few years, and we needed the Big Gulp, then the forty-four-ounce Super Big Gulp, then that was no good, so we created the sixty-four-ounce Double Gulp. Where is our savior Michael Bloomberg when you need him? By the way, did you know that Big Gulps, Super Big Gulps, Double Gulps were exempt from Mr. Bloomberg's NYC ban on sugary drinks? Just thought I would throw that one in there for ya.

But apparently sixty-four ounces was the limit from a practical standpoint. Carrying around anything more than that would have simply been too much exercise because you'd need to curl that behemoth jug to your lips every time you wanted a gulp. Besides it might look just fine for dirty, potty-mouth construction workers to carry that around with them all day, but to urban professional business ladies, it was simply a business fashion faux pas. (Wait, what about a three-liter, smartly designed, and fashionable Big Gulp Camelbak pack? I want royalties on that one, 7-Eleven.) Since sixty-four ounces was the limit, we began packing all that caffeine and other carcinogens we could into a neatly packed can of energy. This is another perfect example of how we created a whole new industry, the "Power Energy Drink Industry," to help us cope because mankind suddenly ain't what it used to be after millions of years of evolution.

Pretty soon, jet lag will be a disorder, then a syndrome, and then a disease. Then cometh plenty of prescription drugs to help us cope with flying from LAX to JFK. I'm sorry. I forgot—jet lag is already a disorder. It has to be classified as a disorder in order for pharmaceutical companies to charge an arm and a leg for their drugs, and of course you then have to take more prescription drugs to deal with all the side effects from the original drug, keeping us smiling every time our 401K Pfizer stock jumps 5 percent.

I know there will be a slew of people screaming and yelling at me because there are people who have genuine phobias or mental disorders or imbalances in their biological chemistry that would cause them to fit into one of these categories. Those people do need prescriptions or therapy to help them cope with these conditions that the rest of us just don't understand. I'm not talking about those few individuals. I'm talking about the rest of us who have begun to make excuses at every turn and run to our doctors for the magic pill to solve all our problems. After all, why should I give my body a normal or reasonable amount of time to adjust when I can simply run to my doctor and take care of it now? And, of course, the doctor is a willing participant in this little social experiment of ours because for him, it's billable hours and kickbacks from the pharmaceutical companies. Why would he think to do otherwise? In the process, we are raising all these disorders and syndromes to the prestigious level of a disease so we can keep the medical industry and our insurance rates at a premium!

The list of new disorders and syndromes out there gets bigger every year. In the previous chapter, we talked about obesity as a disease. Obesity isn't a disease; laziness and weakness are the disease. Obesity is simply the side effect. One of the latest, greatest diseases on the horizon is phantom vibration syndrome (PVS). PVS is when you think your cell phone is vibrating in your pocket, but it's not. Instead of detaching our phones from our bodies for a day or two, or a week, or however long it takes for the vibrating sensation to go away, we run to our beloved doctors for help. How about just turning the damn thing off for an hour or two here and there? I know—that's out of the question because God forbid we miss a text while driving.

For thousands of generations, our forefathers worked harder than we will ever know just to provide the basic necessities for their families. It was their reality, their life, and their daily norm. With all the modern-day conveniences we have to make our lives easier, we can't deal with the slightest distractions or adjustments to our cozy, pretentious lifestyle, including, but not limited to, the changing of the seasons. What does that say about who we are and what we are becoming? I will allow each of you to ponder that question in your own way. As for me, I would say we are becoming a species of wimps who make unjustifiable excuses for our behaviors at every turn. And why should we do otherwise when we have been taught, even as children, that life is a bowl of cherries, we are entitled to be happy, and when we're not, there is a pill to alter our reality and make it all go away? With every decade that goes by, we lower the bar, we lower the standards, and as we do, people are getting weaker and more dependent on artificial stimuli than ever before. We are significantly slipping on the food chain, and it won't be long before we completely slide into the rabbit hole, never to be seen again!

And if you go chasing rabbits,
And you know you're going to fall,
Go ask Alice
When she's ten feet tall.
　　　　　　—Jefferson Airplane, "White Rabbit"

Prozac Nation

"Revised estimates indicate that, among 235,067 adults (in 45 states, the District of Columbia [DC], Puerto Rico, and the US Virgin Islands), 9.1% met the criteria for current depression…including 4.1% who met the criteria for major depression."[1] Translation: approximately one out of ten of us are clinically depressed, and roughly one out of twenty-five are majorly depressed.

What reason do we have to be depressed today? Living in Europe during the bubonic plague that horrifically killed one-third of the population—that was a time to be depressed. The great Irish potato famine of the mid-1800s that wiped out a million folks and displaced another million—that was a time to be depressed. Being Chinese and living in the City of Nanking during the Rape of Nanking—that was a time to be depressed. Being a Jew living in Nazi-occupied Europe during World War II—that was a time to be depressed. Living in Darfur today—that would be a reason to be depressed.

So what do those of us living in the developed world have to be depressed about today? The Cardinals lost the World Series? Our boss is an asshole? Our job sucks? We couldn't get refinanced on our mortgage because we live well beyond our means, and all our credit cards are maxed out? At forty-five, we're suddenly having a midlife crisis and are depressed as ever because our life didn't turn out the way we thought it would. Instead of looking in the mirror, taking responsibility for our mistakes and working to correct them, we blame everyone, including our parents, our spouses, and our kids, for getting in the way of what we might or might not have been.

Please, people! Our modern-day excuses for depression are depressing, and pathetic. The roots of our depression were planted during the self-esteem movement of the early '70s that taught us that life would be wonderful simply because we were special. As we grew up, the specialness of our own benevolence segued right into an entitlement state that said if we can't earn it or be fiscally responsible enough to plan for it, then it should be provided for us because it's our *right* to have whatever we want simply because we are special. And of course, when we started to realize that we aren't so special and life wasn't the bowl of cherries that we were taught it was supposed to be (and there was already a waiting line of people taking advantage of all the entitlements and not nearly as many generous people willing to pay for them), then we discovered, as we had been taught from a very early age, that the next appropriate step was to take plenty of antidepressants to cheer us up. Society taught us a lie that we bought into because we didn't know any better, and now that we're older, instead of denouncing the lie, we just deny it and cover up the truth with the multibillion-dollar-a-year industry of SSRIs.

And why not take the easy way out? As children, we were taught to take drugs when needed, and the need was often. As immature teens, we began to see that the perfect world we were taught to expect was a fairy tale, so we began to experiment with recreational drugs or continue our prescription drug habit or both. As college students, we took our Adderall and uppers to keep awake and focused. As adults, we pop prescription drugs for everything and anything, including ODD, SAD, SWD, PVS, and obesity, just to name a few. Professional sports athletes are so juiced up it's pathetic. But hey, as long as they keep hitting homers and breaking records, life is good because that's what keeps us fans buying tickets and merchandise flying off the shelves. Yes, ladies and gentlemen, we truly have become a Prozac nation.

The electronic and computer age was supposed to make our lives easy and comfortable. What happened? Why all the tears? Why is it that we can't deal with the slightest distractions or inconveniences to our lifestyle? Have we become *too* comfortable in our ways that our expectations now outweigh our reality? And of course, no moss gathers on this societal rolling stone even though it is looking and feeling more and more like a kidney stone.

It seems that when we don't get what we want, we have a tendency to give up, get depressed, and start letting someone else provide for us. And when we *do* get what we want, we want more. We have to keep up with the Joneses. We have to maintain the image because that's what's important to us. And when the image begins to get blurry and is no longer in high definition, we get depressed, which leads to a chemical intervention to help us cope. This intervention oftentimes develops into an addiction to the drugs we're taking or a need to take other drugs to offset the side effects from the original drug. As the movie *Annie Hall* says, "I used to be a heroin addict, now I'm a methadone addict." Thank you, Woody Allen.

A report from the National Institutes of Health, states:

About 11 percent of adolescents have a depressive disorder by age 18 according to the National Comorbidity Survey-Adolescents Supplement (NCS-A)...According to the World Health Organization, major depressive disorder is the leading cause of disability among Americans age 15 to 44...Although antidepressants are generally safe, the US Food and Drug Administration has placed a "black box" warning label – the most serious type of warning – on all antidepressant medications. The warning says there is an increased risk of suicidal thinking or attempts in youth taking antidepressants. Youth and young adults should be closely monitored especially during initial weeks of treatment.[2]

Nothing surprises me anymore, and it certainly doesn't surprise me that "11 percent of adolescents have a depressive disorder by age 18." It also does not surprise me that "major depressive disorder is the leading cause of disability among Americans age 15 to 44." Another main point: "Although antidepressants are generally safe, the US Food and Drug Administration has placed a "black box" warning label – the most serious type of warning – on all antidepressant medications." Great! They're *generally* safe, but not really, is the gist of the matter. And we're handing them out like candy on Halloween.

We, as a society, have nothing to be depressed about. Many times we have discussed how fortunate, yet unappreciative, we are to have and to enjoy all the conveniences that are a part of our daily lives; conveniences that our great-grandfathers could only dream of, if they could imagine them at all. On one hand, we have this wonderfully comfortable world that we have created; on the other hand, we are as depressed as ever. Like a gambling addiction or alcoholism or a drug addiction, we keep chasing things that we believe will bring us happiness, but they don't. So we keep chasing harder and harder, getting more and more depressed. And instead of realizing this, acknowledging this, and taking corrective action to right the wrong, we just cover it up with Dr. Feel Good!

"Sometimes it feels like we're all living in a Prozac nation. The United States of Depression."

—Elizabeth Wurtzel, *Prozac Nation*

My Life Coach

*T*here used to be a saying that went, "When the going gets tough, the tough get going." Today when the going gets tough, the tough take Prozac. When the Prozac doesn't work any longer, they turn to illegal drugs. When that wears off, they begin to blame everyone but themselves. When the finger-pointing no longer works, they drink like fish. And when all else fails, they go out and get themselves a life coach. They spend thousands of dollars to have someone tell them what's important in life and what's worth discarding. They actually pay someone to help them figure out how to juggle their busy schedules and how to make sense of it all.

When I started writing about life coaches, I thought it was going to be a short blurb, perhaps a paragraph at most. Little did I realize this is not just some mundane job description created from the demands of modern-day society, but a thriving one billion dollar a year industry. The International Coach Foundation (ICF)—the leading global coaching organization and professional association for coaches—defines coaching as "partnering with clients in a thought-provoking and creative process that inspires them to maximize their personal and professional potential."[1] If that doesn't sound like the greatest yuppie-inspired, politically correct, gobbledygook bullshit I have ever heard, then I don't know what is.

And if you're down on your luck and your midlife crisis is getting the best of you, but you don't want to spend thousands of dollars attending a weeklong seminar having a life coach tell you what a fuckup you are, then for $650 you can make an exciting career change, become a life coach yourself, and tell others what fuckups *they* are. The Fowler International Academy of Professional Coaching is just one of many fine organizations in the billion-dollar-a-year industry of life coaching that will help you attain your goals. For a measly $650 and just twenty hours, you can become a certified professional coach (CPC). And if you're feeling really ambitious, you can fork over $3,997 and sign up for Fowler's thirty-hour course to become a certified master business coach (MBC).[2] It's hard to imagine why anyone in their right mind would want to waste a couple hundred thousand dollars and six years of college on a master's of business administration (MBA), or a degree in psychiatry, when one week and $3,997 later you can have your MBC and have all the stressed-out MBAs and shrinks come to you for help.

About ten years ago, when I was in my early forties, I was sitting in a job interview for a middle-level managerial position, and one of the interviewers asked me, "What is your greatest accomplishment?"

"My kids," I told him. He was surprised, as that was not the answer he was expecting. I went on to explain that I had more time, money, and resources invested in them than I did in my house, my savings, and my 401K combined, and the investment was paying off nicely. My kids, and subsequently my grandkids, are *my* life coaches. They help me keep it all in perspective, constantly teaching me and reinforcing the things that are truly important in life and what's worth discarding.

By the way, I got the job.

Going Postal

I remember standing in line at the post office waiting to buy stamps, breathing very slowly and methodically—in through my nose, out through my barely parted lips. It was about a month after September 11, 2001, and right smack in the middle of the anthrax mailing attacks that had already killed five people and seriously infected many others. Aside from the strange sensation of uncertainty and despair of the 9/11 attacks, this was the first time I felt personally threatened in my own paranoid way. So there I was, breathing slowly and methodically, trying to limit my intake of airborne particles, as if that was somehow going to save my life if, in fact, there was anthrax in the air. Looking back, I have a feeling that walking in with a canary on my shoulder would have given me a better chance.

A 2010 OSHA report on workplace violence, states:

Homicide is currently the fourth-leading cause of fatal occupational injuries in the United States...Homicide is the leading cause of death for women in the workplace...Nearly 2 million American workers report having been victims of workplace violence each year. Unfortunately, many more cases go unreported. The truth is, workplace violence can strike anywhere, anytime, and no one is immune.[1]

That's a powerful statement: "Workplace violence can strike anywhere, anytime, and no one is immune." And like everything else that we allow to progressively get worse, workplace violence has spread to every faction of society.

A year after 9/11 and the anthrax mailings, I was pumping gas in a suburb of Washington, DC. I was up there visiting friends for the weekend, and as I pumped my gas, that same feeling of helplessness and vulnerability came over me. The DC sniper shootings were in full swing, and as the gas pumped, I found myself washing my windows, which I never do, and bending down pretending to tie my shoes or pick up something off the ground. I was moving about unnecessarily, doing anything I could to keep out of the crosshairs of Lee Boyd Malvo and his buddy, John Allen Muhammad. It was the first time in my life I began to routinely feel a sense of vulnerability and paranoia as I went about my normal daily activities. I had a feeling that I was just not safe anymore, regardless of where I was or what I was doing. Whether at work, or going and coming from work, or eating lunch at a restaurant, or going out to a movie theater, or a concert, or getting on a plane, things were different from that time forward. I looked at people differently, with a heightened sense of suspicion and awareness of what was or what might be going on around me. As time went by, I began to forget about those societal woes, and my paranoia began to wane. Then there was another mass shooting, another stabbing, another biological weapon scare, another bombing, and they were all way too close to home.

And what does society do about it? We approach it the same way we approach school violence: convoluted solutions to serious problems that only address the symptoms, not the root causes of the issues at hand.

We used to have cameras on the exterior of our place of business to collect evidence of any perpetrators who may break in after-hours. Today there are cameras everywhere inside and out, except perhaps the bathrooms, and it wouldn't surprise me if the head of IT got busted for putting spy cameras in the ladies' stalls. We have street cams and traffic cams that catch accidents and people running red lights. We have cameras in restaurants, malls, movie theaters, bus stations, train stations, subways, airports, and on the sidewalks of Main Street, USA. We have added security personnel everywhere. We have to take our shoes off to get on a plane. We have Google Earth that can zoom in on your home like an alien spaceship and take pictures of you leaving your house with your mistress while your wife is visiting her terminally sick mother in Toledo. We have dashboard cams on police cars, and now more and more private individuals are putting dashboard cams in their own personal vehicles. Cops now have license plate reader cameras mounted to the trunks of their cruisers. We have our government tapping our phones, reading our e-mails, reviewing our texts and our tweets at their discretion. We have more and more drones patrolling overhead to keep us safe, and I'm not talking about Afghanistan. And every person in the civilized (I say that loosely) world has a camera on their cell phone to capture everything and anything going on among us. Because of our inability to adequately fix, or even address, the problem, we are becoming a police state, and Big Brother is watching *everything*!

And although everyone is being watched, we can't *profile* anyone because that would be a violation of someone's rights. It doesn't matter that an overwhelming majority of a particular demographic commits an overwhelming majority of specific crimes—we can't *profile* them. So what do we do? Instead of giving a little more scrutiny to the suspicious-looking guy at the airport who is wearing sunglasses and a hoodie on a 100 degree August afternoon, we get the eighty-five-year-old grandma who is traveling from Yuma to Kansas City to visit the great-grand kids, and we pull her out of her wheelchair, giving her a cavity search and a pap smear. This is nothing more than reverse profiling so we can prove to the rest of the world, regardless of what the statistics and the facts show, that we are treating *everyone* equally and fairly. If that's the case, why doesn't law enforcement get rid of all criminal analysis personnel whose job it is to do behavioral profiles to find out what demographic and what type of people are committing these crimes to begin with? Oh, that's right, if we got rid of them then CSI would have to go off the air, and God forbid, we would ever allow that to happen. So let's keep the profilers to give us the stats we need, then turn around and tell the cops walking the beat that they can't use this information because it's, profiling.

Human beings are at an evolutionary turning point, the beginning of a tightly controlled, yet completely ineffective, and dysfunctional police state where Big Brother is watching everything. The more he watches, the more of our civil liberties are being stripped away until someday in the not-too-distant future we all become eighty-five-year-old grandmas from Yuma. And, of course, it's all for our own good! Civilization can no longer behave in a civilized manner, so Big Brother has to look out for us. But who's watching Big Brother?

There was a recent Los Angeles story (October 2013) about a father and his fifteen-year-old son who went to buy a cell phone from an ad that they saw on Craigslist. Apparently the whole thing was a setup, and the father was robbed and fatally shot in front of his son. That story, sadly, is hardly news anymore, but what I did find distressing was how it was reported by nbcnews.com: "The slaying happened just hours after the Los Angeles Police Department announced that there had not been a homicide in the city in 10 days and 10 nights—the longest streak since 2010...'Homicides do happen,' LAPD spokesman Cleon Joseph said. 'We're happy we had a streak of this nature.'"[2] What a bizarre public statement for the LAPD spokesman to say, *"Homicides do happen, we're happy we had a streak of this nature."* If that isn't a sign of what's to come, then I don't know what is.

Societal and workplace violence is a problem that is only getting worse, and our response to the problem is to add more cameras, more security guards, and more law enforcement officers. In another ten years or so, we will be engaged in a great fiscal debate as to where we are going to get the money to add more cameras, more security guards, and more law enforcement officers. Ten years after that, we will be engaged in another great fiscal debate as to where we are going to get more money to add more and more...

The US Post Office can no longer take credit for the abundance of workplace violence because it has now spread to every faction of our lives. People are going office building, going retail store, going gas station, going shopping mall, going to the movies, going fast-food restaurant, going to school, going to church, going Craigslist, and, yes, going postal. If you ask me, I'd say we're going, going, gone!

Barbie

I think it's hilarious (hilarious in the context of keeping yourself from going insane) that it is now an issue that Barbie is not anatomically correct and that her 39-18-33 figure promotes unrealistic expectations of what women should look like. Don't we have anything better to worry about? I mean, on one hand, society promotes these unrealistic expectations by exploiting, even encouraging, plastic surgery: Botox lips, breast implants, liposuction, tummy tucks, and facial cosmetic surgery. We're consumed with looking young and beautiful, not to mention what's hot and what's not in the fashion and cosmetic world, and then we turn around and blame Barbie for our misconstrued societal woes!

On May 21, 2012, the *Huffington Post* published the results from a survey conducted by the United Kingdom discount website, myvouchercodes.com.[1] The survey asked 1,100 women between the ages of eighteen and twenty-five, if they would trade their IQ's for bigger breasts. A staggering 41 percent of those women stated that they *would* rather have bigger breasts than a higher IQ.

If you stop and consider that one-quarter, or perhaps, one-third of those women were already well endowed and perfectly happy with the size of their breasts, then that would bring the figure of all other respondents to well over 50 percent.

According to Huffington, the survey went on to state some other interesting results:

Forty-nine percent of the respondents believed that being "attractive" would also help a woman in her career...57 percent of the women said they thought men would be "more interested" in them romantically if they had bigger breasts and 59 percent said they thought that, when looking for a relationship, men valued the appearance of a woman more so than her intelligence. Overall, a whopping 79 percent of all women surveyed felt that they were judged more by their appearance than by their intelligence.

And this is Barbie's fault? Barbie is responsible for the vogue bikini waxes, the anal bleaching's, and the scrotum de-wrinkling? First of all, kids who play with Barbie just want to play with Barbie and aren't consumed with her anatomical imperfections (or perfections, depending on your, the glass is half empty or half full, perspective). And the adults who are making an issue out of all this? Well, if you're a grown-up and still obsessed with Barbie's anatomical features, I'm sure you can find a very good shrink in your geographical area that would love to discuss the matter with you.

The survey above is a sad reminder of what we see in an individual, what we value as a society, and what we are becoming as a species. And the trend shows no sign of stopping or even slowing down. Adults are the ones who need to grow up and decide if we're going to keep creating and glorifying these real-life Barbie's or if we are going to get back to the basics, open our eyes, and start appreciating and admiring true and natural beauty, both outer and inner. In the meantime, leave Barbie alone! You perverts!

Feminism at Its Finest

I didn't write the rules of estrogen and testosterone, God did. If you're a Darwinist, evolution did. If you're an atheist and believe that the evolution of all life throughout the cosmos is just a crapshoot, then so be it. But regardless of what you believe, life is the way it is. I didn't write it, and neither did you, it's just the way it is.

Males, by virtue of testosterone, are the hunters, and women, by virtue of estrogen, are the gatherers. That's not to say women can't be CEOs, or fly combat missions for the military, or climb Mount Everest, or achieve any other greatness they aspire to in life. But it does say that by the natural law of all living things, there are certain biological conditions that are innate within, and unique to, the sexes. And this is the point where the steadfast feminists of the '60s took a turn for the worse and steered the ship into the iceberg.

There are reasons why male Bighorn rams smash their heads together to fight for who will mate with the female, not vice versa. And there is a reason why, when they're done fighting over the females, the males mount the females, not vice versa. (I haven't done any research on this, but I'm pretty sure it was cowgirls who first invented the "cowboy position" and the "reverse cowboy position," not rams, or any other species for that matter.) There is a reason why the female has the children, not vice versa. And there is a reason why the female stays home gathering, with the kids suckling at her breasts, while the male is out hunting for food and not vice versa.

No human made these "laws of nature" that take place in almost every living species on the face of the earth (snails excluded, of course), and yet for some reason, the modern-day feminist feels the need to fix it. She feels that males of the human species need to be fixed, both literally and figuratively. The rest of mother nature is just fine, but we Homo sapien males need to be neutered of our masculinity!

Since the beginning of mankind, women have had a support role in civilization; they have been the gatherers, if you will. Now I'm no doctor or sociologist, but if I had to guess, I would say that the reason this condition existed for millions of years would be: a) women are the ones who actually give birth to the babies, not the men and; b) women are the ones who feed (breastfeed) the young ones, not the men. And if the mothers were well-to-do and didn't want to breastfeed the child, or were unable to breastfeed the child, then they found another woman to be their wet nurse, not a man. All the while, the man was out hunting, killing, looking after his family's well-being, protecting the cave, its stone furniture possessions, and the accessories of cave paintings on the wall. Then one day, after millions of years of evolution, human infant formula became commercially available, and women had an option. Next there came the birth control pill, and women had even more options. Next thing you know, we started hearing women were victims of a male-dominated society. Victims of what? Evolution? Then we started hearing a new word—"sexism." Then we started hearing that women weren't Miss or Mrs. anymore, they were Ms. And from that point forward, man was looked upon as an evil, gender-repressive SOB. (I have actually heard so-called feminists refer to men as SOBs. Before using this acronym, I would like to make a recommendation to all feminists out there: make sure you understand what the "B" in SOB stands for because you are doing your cause more harm than good and showing significant ignorance in the process of using this acronym.)

From the early 1800s until the 1960s, the feminist movement accomplished some pretty amazing things. The nineteenth amendment gave women the right to vote. World War II proved that women could be a valuable asset in the workforce and that they could do the same job as men with equally proficient results. After World War II and into the early '60s, the feminist movement fought for equal rights and equal pay in the workplace. Those were significant accomplishments that brought women to the forefront of equality in American culture.

But then the radical feminists of the '60s (or postfeminist, or modern feminist, or postmodern feminist, or gender feminist, or equity feminist, or liberal feminist, or whatever other kind of feminist you wish to be associated with) decided it was payback time for centuries of repression and "gender racism," and decided to take things into their own hands. They burned their bras and proclaimed their emancipation of men. They turned on, tuned in, and dropped out of the conventional ways that women had lived for millennium. Casual sex at a time of their choosing was now preferable over the constraints of a serious, committed relationship. Feminists were now liberated from the restraints of marriage and the notion of "till death do us part." The burden of bearing and raising children, with or without a man, was now a thing of the past as a women could now custom-tailor a family of her choosing when and where she decided. The ripple effect, the unintended consequences, and in some cases, intended consequences, of this payback are: single-parent households; overall drop in birthrate; significant drop in the birthrate of educated women; significant rise in divorce rate; fewer male parental role models for kids to emulate; more and more kids being taught and raised in day cares; less parental supervision of kids, to the point where we had to invent yet another phrase—"quality time"; and the list goes on. And of course each of those concerns have consequences of their own, creating a wave of societal woes that have ingrained themselves so deeply into society that it will take forceps to get them out.

Contemporary feminism isn't entirely responsible for all those societal and family woes, but it certainly has its hand in the cookie jar and, in some cases, has played a significant role.

In the end, modern feminists are just like the bulk of society— they want to have their cake and eat it too. They want to be treated as equals, but when the time comes, they still expect men to go down with the ship. They want to be left with their independence, but still expect men to open doors for them or help them with their coats. Modern-day feminism is nothing more than a faction of the "me" generation. All they really care about is, "What's important to me?"

The days of the Susan B. Anthony feminist are gone. The days of the Rosie the Riveter feminist are gone. The days of wine and roses are gone, and the days of "sexism," "Ms.," and "quality time" are here to stay. Get used to it, you SOBs! It's payback time!

"Mama's got a squeeze box. Daddy never sleeps at night!"
—The Who, "Squeeze Box"

Reality TV—Reality? Please!

*I*think we can all kneel, bow our heads, and give thanks to Jerry Springer for starting the reality TV phenomenon that has infected our society like an airborne bubonic plague. You can't blame Jerry for this; you can only give him the credit. The blame for making him successful and launching this modern-day, incurable disease lies on *our* shoulders. It's a societal epidemic of the people, by the people, and for the people.

Jerry started out in the afternoons, only to be watched by overweight, trailer trash moms in curlers. As time passed, Jerry moved later into the afternoon and the incurable disease metastasized into *Maury*, *The Steve Wilkos Show*, *Ricki Lake*, *The Jeremy Kyle Show*, *The Rosie O'Donnell Show*, and *Dr. Phil*—shows so great that they were all named after their pompous, egotistical hosts. And it really didn't matter what time they were on because instead of technology finding a cure for this plague, it just gave us TiVo, so we could watch it over and over again at any time of the day or night. Through the modern miracle of technology, we could record those shows while we were busy working jobs we hated just so we could buy more crap that we didn't need. And if that wasn't good enough, we made sure there was enough to go around in syndication for posterity.

The summer of 2012 was a very special ten-year anniversary for me. No, it wasn't ten years since I quit smoking or drinking and beating my wife. It wasn't my wedding anniversary or a decade since I beat cancer. It was something much more profound than that. It was the ten-year jubilee since I stopped watching television. And I didn't *just* stop watching television. I unplugged my television from the surge protector, picked it up in my own two arms, carried it to the second-floor balcony of my home, and tossed it over the railing to the awaiting concrete sidewalk below. Have you ever seen the movie *Office Space?* Remember that scene where all the guys are in a grassy field, taking turns on the office copy/fax machine with baseball bats? That was something that I could definitely relate to, and tossing that idiot box and watching it smash into a thousand pieces made me feel, for one brief moment in time, like a movie star.

Saturday, July 13th, 2002, 2:35 p.m. Location: Second-floor family room of my house. There I was, kicked back in my Baralounger, TV remote in hand. Pointing, clicking, and staring at my twenty-seven inch bulky, old-fashioned television, scanning, in command fashion, the 122 channels of my cable package. It had become a Saturday routine of mine, as I'm sure it was the routine of millions of others. A way to relax and de-stress. Back in the day (my childhood), we had three TV channels, all in black & white, and two other fuzzy channels that typically required the manipulation of the "rabbit ears" on top the TV for better reception (high definition—the early years). There were five channels in all. And the amazing thing was you could always find something entertaining to watch, unless, of course, as Jeff Foxworthy so eloquently put it, "If the president was on, your night was shot."

And there I was, thirty-something years later, pointing, staring, and clicking away at my 122 channels, trying to find something, anything, worth watching; surfing through my eight different sports channels, nine news channels, four cooking channels, four government/educational channels, and six different HBO channels including HBO Latino. And let's not forget QVC, Jewelry TV, Pentagon Channel, Jewish Channel, and the Weather Channel. There used to be a time when we would sit around and talk about the weather. Now we sit around and watch it on TV. One can only imagine the possibilities had I coughed up another $19.99 per month for the cable "premium package!"

Even the few channels that I did enjoy watching—A&E, TLC, The History Channel, and Discovery—were becoming saturated with mindless shows devoid of any substance. And why was this happening? To increase ratings and to capture a larger market in an industry whose audience's taste for anything intellectual in nature was capitulating to the contrary.

In my research to see how this topic has evolved over the last ten years, I have discovered that things have only succumbed to further ruin. A&E used to stand for "Arts & Entertainment," where you might catch a glimpse of Leonard Bernstein conducting the New York Philharmonic in a performance of *West Side Story* or perhaps Wynton Marsalis performing a charity jazz concert with Sarah Vaughan and Sonny Rollins on the Santa Monica Pier. Today A&E's most popular lineup consists of shows such as *Barter Kings, Hoarders, Dog the Bounty Hunter, Storage Wars, Storage Wars: Texas* (as if one storage war isn't enough), *Intervention, Billy the Exterminator, Gene Simmons: Family Jewels, Parking Wars,* and *American Hoggers.* My spell-checker doesn't even recognize the word "hoggers," and the description of the show in the online cable network guide reads, "American Hoggers follows the Campbell family and their struggle to rescue Texas residents and ranches from the devastating chaos caused by millions of invasive wild boars." Did I miss something? Does A&E now stand for "Assholes & Etcetera"? *Parking Wars?* A show about meter maids! Seriously?

The other used-to-be intellectual channels aren't any better. TLC boasts shows such as *Nineteen Kids and Counting, I Found the Gown, United Bates of America, DC Cupcakes, Toddlers & Tiaras, Cake Boss, Extreme Couponing, Say Yes to the Dress, What Not to Wear, Long Island Medium, My Big Fat Gypsy Wedding*, and *My Big Fat American Gypsy Wedding* (as if one fat gypsy wasn't enough). The online TLC network guide describes the show *Here Comes Honey Boo Boo* as such: "Take an inside look into Alana's world where the six-year-old pageant sensation proves that she is more than just a Go-Go Juice-drinking beauty queen." I actually forced myself through half an episode of this show. Maybe it's just me and maybe I'm out of touch with *reality*, but I just can't wrap my cerebral cortex around the fact that this is a hit show. And if I want to learn something about how to make cupcakes, or how to maximize my return on grocery store coupons, or the latest fashion advice, or how to shop for a wedding gown, I have this thing called the Internet and the World Wide Web to assist me. I don't need episode after episode, season after season, year after year in syndication to learn the tricks of the cupcake trade, thank you very much.

And just in case you can't get enough in thirty minutes, The History Channel now runs back-to-back-to-back episodes of *Pawn Stars, Ice Road Truckers, Cajun Pawn Stars, Swamp People*, and *Big Shrimpin'*. Yes, you can get anywhere from two to four hours of all the backwoods, Creole-redneck alligator hunting you could possibly pray for. It appears that the Discovery Channel might be the last holdout of anything meaningful and halfway educational with a lineup of *Mythbusters, Survivorman, Discovery News, Dirty Jobs, Frozen Planet, Human Planet*, and *Man vs. Wild*.

When the Romans got bored and needed to raise the stakes in the entertainment arena, they began sacrificing Christians and slaves in the most gruesome and horrific ways, jeering and cheering from their box seats in the Coliseum. Today we up the ante by sitting on our asses and watching reality TV. I'm not sure which is worse. I suppose if you were lazy enough, you could sit around all day and watch two to four hours of professional wrestling and MMA, while fantasizing that you were at the Colosseum two thousand years ago, jeering and cheering at the HD flat screen, although I really hate to give anyone any ideas here.

Reality TV has become the staple crop of mainstream television entertainment. There is nothing spontaneous or real about it, and the more we spend our evenings and weekends immersing ourselves in this meaningless, mindless, sedative activity, as opposed to watching or doing something creative and constructive, the more we become it. We become more like *Cheaters, 16 and Pregnant, Bridezillas, Real Housewives of [you name the county], Teen Mom, Jersey Shore, Toddlers & Tiaras, Half-Pint Brawlers, Dance Moms, The Bachelor, The Bachelorette, EX-treme Dating, My Big Fat Obnoxious Fiancé, Boy Meets Boy, Queer Eye For The Straight Guy, Wife Swap, Mob Wives, Keeping Up with the Kardashians, Snoop Dog Father Hood,* and the list goes on.

And so it was, ten years ago, I surfed and surfed until I just snapped. I couldn't stand it any longer, and there she went—over the railing, onto the concrete sidewalk below, and into a thousand pieces. A feeling of unbridled elation swept over me like the birth of my first child. About six months later, I went out and bought another TV. Not a flat screen, but another big bulky hunk of a TV with a VHS and DVD player, just so I could watch a good movie from time to time. But to this day, I still do not have "television"—no cable, no satellite dish harmoniously and aesthetically mounted to the roof of my house, no rabbit ears on top of the idiot box. No "television," just a TV.

I believe most reality TV shows can be summed up in one sobering story that occurred involving the show *Extreme Makeover,* a show that I'm sure most people would consider innocent enough. It helps people overcome adversities by improving their self-esteem, and, as a result, the quality of their lives. The following excerpt is from a story by Michelle Caruso, published in the September 18, 2005 edition of the *New York Daily News*:

> The producers of "Extreme Makeover" promised Deleese Williams "a Cinderella-like" fix for a deformed jaw, crooked teeth, droopy eyes and tiny boobs that would "transform her life and destiny." But when the ABC reality show dumped the Texas mom the night before the life-changing plastic surgeries, it shattered her family's dream and triggered her sister Kellie McGee's suicide, says a bombshell lawsuit filed in L.A. Superior Court. As part of the premakeover hype, producers coaxed McGee and other family members to trash Williams's looks on videotape, the suit alleges. When they suddenly pulled the plug on the project, and the promised "Hollywood smile like Cindy Crawford," a guilt-ridden McGee fell apart. "Kellie could not live with the fact that she had said horrible things that hurt her sister. She fell to pieces. Four months later, she ended her life with an overdose of pills, alcohol and cocaine," said Wesley Cordova, a lawyer for Williams.[1]

Now that, my friends, is reality!

Inquiring Minds
Want to Know

$\mathcal{S}$ ometime in November 2011, I was standing in the ten-items-or-less, not-so-express line at my local supermarket. In a moment like that, there is not much we humans can do except play on our cell phones, which I don't do, or people watch, which I hate to do. That leaves the only real option—read the covers of dozens upon dozens of tabloid magazines, which include *US Weekly*, *National Enquirer*, *National Examiner*, *The Globe*, *Sun*, *Self*, *Star*, *People*, *In Touch Weekly*, *Life & Style*, *M*, *Jet*, *Juicy*, *Soap Opera Digest*, *Teen Vogue*, *OK! Magazine*, and *Celebrity Hairstyles*, to name a few.

I was oddly embarrassed for simply being in the same proximity of such sensational trash, as if I were a juvenile, guilty of some stupendous crime and waiting for my parents at the police station. I tried not to be obvious as my peripheral scanned the journalistic toxic waste loosely stacked on each side of me; a sight that would make William Randolph Hearst himself drool with envy. Suddenly something caught my eye, my attention, and then my curiosity, as if Citizen Kane had subliminally planted it there himself. The headline of the November 14, 2011 edition of *US Weekly* read, "Kim Kardashian, Inside Their Final Days." My right brain begged me to pick it up, oozing with uncontrollable curiosity. My left brain winced, saying, "Don't touch that," wondering how many people had handled it, like a dollar bill still in circulation from the '80s. Now, I have to take a moment and put this into historical perspective. This was before Kimmy hooked up with Kanye (pronounced Con-yeah, in case any of you didn't know), and she was in her relationship-of-the-moment with Kris Humphries. Kimmy and Kris were married for seventy-two days before they parted ways, and so the headline "Kim Kardashian, Inside Their Final Days" was odd to me. They were only married for seventy-two days to begin with before they separated, so what were *the final days*? The last month? The last week? The last forty-eight hours? Did they even try? Don't answer that!

Sometime later, I read in a breaking tabloid story that, according to Kimmy, the reason for the split was "irreconcilable differences." But that's the artificial times we live in, isn't it? We get married, we give it a couple months, and then if it doesn't work out, screw it! And, of course, the jury is still out concerning whether or not the marriage was just one big publicity stunt in order to grab more publicity. It's all about protecting your *brand*, your *image*, and your *dynasty*! And now little Kimmy is having a kid out of wedlock with Kanye before her divorce to Kris is final, and we just can't seem to get enough of this exhilarating tabloid news.

This is a classic example of how pretentious and superficial we have become and what is really important to us, as this is not an isolated story, but one that is becoming the status quo. And the real Shakespearian tragedy in all of this is that we don't see it as a tragedy at all, but as entertainment. We humans can't get enough of this sensationalism, and whether it's true or not, we don't seem to care as long as we get our gossip that we can text, tweet, e-mail, post on Facebook, and talk about at work when we are supposed to be filling out the TPS reports. And what about all the trophy children being born into these fairy-tale Hindenburg stories that are just waiting to explode, like Kim and Kanye's new little one?

I like to call it the Gosselin syndrome. Here you have the reality TV show *Jon & Kate Plus 8*, where your private life and your kids are paraded around in the public eye in classic Hollywood fashion. One day, mommy and daddy don't love each other anymore, so of course they just bail out of the relationship, and the show is canceled. End of story, right? Wrong! Let's regroup, change the name of the show to *Kate Plus 8*, and focus on Kate as a divorced, single mother raising the kids on her own. Absolutely no consideration for the kids, their feelings, their privacy, or anything else except the sales and the profit. Let's exploit the kids at their own expense for the sake of ratings. And who can blame the producers when *we're* the ones watching week after week. My inquiring mind can't wait to see how those eight turn out!

Thanks to Kim Kardashian, all her Hollywood friends, and the dumbing down of the human race, the popular celebrity and entertainment magazine *US Weekly* has a *weekly* circulation in the United States of almost 2 million copies, for a total monthly circulation of 7,839,136.[1] In my search to find an academic comparison, I chose the *National Geographic* magazine. Founded in 1888, *National Geographic* has become a home staple for history, geography, and world culture, and is one of the best-selling intellectual magazines in the world. Unfortunately for the human race, *National Geographic* only sells 4,001,937 copies per month in the United States, a mere 53 percent compared to *Us Weekly*.[1] *Cosmopolitan* and *Maxim* collectively sell more than five million copies monthly in the US market.[1] *Star* magazine sells 3.1 million.[1] *The Globe* sells in excess of 1 million.[2] Even with the huge expansion in the tabloid magazine market over the past couple of decades, the good ol' tried and true *National Enquirer* still sells 2.1 million copies per month, a circulation of more than half that of the *National Geographic*.[3]

Once again, leave it to mankind to create an industry void of any journalistic integrity, yet sells tens of millions of magazines each and every month and grosses hundreds of millions of dollars every year just so we can get our gossip on. It's no surprise that human intelligence is on the decline when tabloid journalism and reality TV are exploding in popularity. There seems to be a very distinct and obvious correlation between the two.

Being on the cover (or even inside on page seventeen) of a tabloid magazine used to be a joke, something that was frowned upon and laughed at. It was sensationalism about someone famous getting caught red-handed screwing an alien, and I'm not talking about Arnold Schwarzenegger banging his illegal alien au pair. But nowadays, making the tabloids is cool. It's an honor. Its press coverage worthy of furthering a career as the tabloids fly off the racks.

Mr. Hearst, you missed your day in the sun. You showed up too early and missed the golden age of journalistic tabloidism in all its grandeur! Imagine what your castle, or your "ranch" as you so lovingly referred to it, would look like had it been built with the greed, sensationalism, and mindless stupidity of today's society!

ROSEBUD!!!!!!!

The Social Disease

Social media is one of the classic examples of how we humans have made a mockery out of a beautiful thing. When Al Gore invented the Internet in 1978,[1] it was a marvel to be reckoned with, like the modern-day equivalent of the laying of the transatlantic cable in the mid-1800s.

With the information superhighway and the World Wide Web at our fingertips, man could now go where no man had gone before. No more going to the music store to buy sheet music for *Purple Haze* just to confirm that Jimmy wasn't saying, "Excuse me while I kiss this guy." Now we can sit at home in our jammies with our cup of joe and type in "lyrics purple haze" on our computer, and in five seconds, the answer magically appears. And when it comes to driving, there's no more arguing over the roadmap on the way to grandma's for Christmas. Just turn on your GPS and punch in your destination just in time to hear the lady say, "Make your first legal U-turn."

Yes, the Internet has brought some pretty amazing technological advances to this world, and how do we return the favor? Instead of using it to further our knowledge and understanding of who we are in an effort to make the world a better place, we use it to further our video game addiction: "Dr. Kimberly Young runs the nation's first and only inpatient Internet addiction center. She said just like folks with drug or alcohol addictions, people go through detox—only this one is a digital detox."[2] Here is yet another man-made industry we have created to help us cope with the man-made societal problems we have created. The article continues, "She sees it all the time at the center, a 10 day program that costs people $14,000 out of pocket. Insurance companies aren't covering "Internet addiction" treatment yet." Not yet, but I don't get the impression that this is a problem that's going away anytime soon and I am willing to bet it will only get worse. "The majority of patients she sees are gamers, the 20-somethings who spend up to 12 hours a day playing games like World of Warcraft and Call of Duty." Internet addiction is nothing more than a lack of discipline, period. But like everything else in this world of ours, we have created excuses for our behavior in an effort to legitimize it. It won't be long before Internet addiction is categorized as a disease and then nationalized health care will foot the bill. In the meantime, you would think that the price tag of fourteen thousand dollars out of pocket for a meager ten days of intervention would get people to wake up and start making some corrections to their lifestyle. You would think! But the days of self-discipline and personal responsibility are over, my friends.

The article goes on to say, "She also sees patients with diagnosed addictions to cyber dating and online gambling." "Addictions to cyber dating" was new to me. If you're addicted to cyber dating, then you must be a miserable date. I thought that the whole idea of Internet dating was to find a compatible mate. If you're addicted to it, what does that say about you? I bet you forgot to mention that you are addicted to cyber dating in your online profile, didn't you? And if people meet their one true love online, then it only stands to reason that today's cowardly norm for ending a relationship is to breakup online by texting or e-mailing the individual, then letting the rest of the world know by posting it on Facebook and Twitter just to make sure they have everyone covered and informed that they are, once again, available.

I suppose the positive side of online dating is that it weeds out a lot of BS and psychos, linking people with common interests so you don't waste the next two months of your life finding out it's not going to work (unless of course you're addicted to it, then that becomes the whole point of it, I presume). This, of course, is a very big and very risky assumption—that the person you are interested in is being honest on his or her online profile and isn't a psycho. Let's face it: I don't know many psychos (and I know a lot of psychos) who think they're psychos. It's always the other guy. After all, you never see ads saying, "Sadistic, psychopath, woman beater, ISO submissive bitch for good times. No freaks please." No, you never see those, do you? It's always, "Tall, handsome, physically fit man of good humor...blah, blah, blah!" (Actually, I'm not being on the up and up on this one. I just don't want to give any young impressionable minds out there, if there are any left, any ideas. But if you go to Craigslist, or a number of other shady dating sites, you will find ads like the one I just mentioned.) Now I know why comedienne Maria Bamford refers to the dating website eharmony. com as e-harming-me.com.

No one has time to develop meaningful relationships anymore. The computer age that was supposed to make our lives so much easier has been successful in expanding our workload tenfold to the point where we don't have time to get to know someone personally or intellectually. Instead the question has become, "What's the quickest, fastest way to fall in infatuation, mistake it for love, get hitched, get divorced, tell everyone about it on Facebook, and then move on?" As Tyler Durden puts it in the movie *Fight Club*, we are becoming a society of "single-serving friends." When people sit next to you on the plane, you exchange pleasantries like "Where are you going?" "What do you do?" "Nice to meet you!" and "Take care!" And then we're off to hook up with our next new single-serving friend, all while posting a one-sentence comment on Facebook about the wonderful single-serving friend we just met on the airplane.

A friend once told me that a friend is someone you haven't seen or talked to in years who calls you up out of the blue in the middle of the night and tells you they need you to drive six hours and bail them out of jail. Without hesitation, you jump out of bed, kiss your wife on the cheek, tell her you'll explain later, get in your car, and you do it. That's friendship. Robert De Niro's portrayal of Michael Vronsky in the movie *The Deer Hunter*, that's friendship, that's love! Two marines in a foxhole in Afghanistan who wouldn't think twice about laying down their lives for each other—that's friendship, that's love! The quintessential modern-day true friend invites you over on Sunday afternoon to watch the game and shares his home-brewed beer, and then has an affair with your wife when you're off to Orlando for your next business conference. That's modern-day friendship, that's love!

And let's not forget about kids hooking up online with pedophiles, sex addicts, and murderers. Those perverts are certainly posting honest information about themselves. And, of course, there's teenagers "sexting" online (another wonderful modern-age word/issue that has popped up as a result of our abuse of technology), which certainly doesn't help. Even the FBI, the ICE (US Immigration and Customs Enforcement), the NCMEC (National Center for Missing & Exploited Children), and the HSI (Homeland Security Investigations), just to name a few, are all very concerned about the increase in sexual exploitation of minors online.[3] While researching this topic, I came across an online article titled, "Experts increasingly worried about 'sextortion' of minors online." At the top of the webpage was an ad for Cialis. If that isn't a sign of the times we live in, I don't know what is.

Yes, ladies and gentlemen, we feel entitled to our toys don't we? We feel entitled to them without accepting responsibility for our actions or even the basic necessity to use them safely. How many innocent people have been killed or had life-altering injuries as a result of someone texting while driving? And we still can't help ourselves, can we? I bet it would help curtail the problem if we made a law that said if you ever injure a person as a result of texting while driving, you can never, ever use a cell phone again. Ever! But of course we can't do that because it would be an infringement on someone's civil liberties, I'm sure.

The Internet has also brought some amazing conveniences to our lives, such as the ease of paying bills and making purchases online. But with every advance, there are a host of consequences that come with it. One such consequence would be yet another man-made industry called cyber security. Identity theft is a booming business that everyone, from the individual to big business to the federal government, has to be concerned with. As if the fifty to one hundred work e-mails I routinely get every day aren't bad enough, I now have to receive and respond to yet another e-mail from my cyber security company every time I use my credit card or purchase something online. Not to mention the additional $19.99 plus taxes and surcharges I have to pay each and every month for the privilege of this piece of mind. Peace of mind, that is, when I'm not worrying about which major retailer I routinely patronize just got hacked.

Getting an education online is another wonderful convenience for stay-at-home moms and people with physical limitations. But with more and more young people pursuing an online education, I can't help but wonder what the long-term impact will be. Young people today are already socially disengaged more than ever, and now they can get a master's degree without even leaving the house for the next five to six years. Zoloft, here we come!

The blog is another wonderful concept with a horrible reality. Let's post a site where people who have no idea what they're talking about can hide behind a screen and a fictitious name, and blurt out every opinion they have about everything they pretend to know about.

Facebook is the heart and soul of our social decline. It's not a network. It's a disease and an addiction of monumental proportions. It's where we congregate to post mundane and meaningless tidbits about our moment-to-moment pathetic lives—tidbits about what we had for dinner or how bad it sucks to be stuck in traffic on a Friday afternoon, as if this is something new that no one else knows about. (I suppose I should be grateful that they're texting when they're stuck in traffic and not going sixty miles per hour down the interstate.) Facebook is where we go to read, reply, poke, and "like" what other people had for breakfast or comment in solidarity about our traffic dilemmas. These are single-serving comments to our host of single-serving friends. And what about all the people who have lost jobs or have not been hired for jobs because of all the bullshit they have posted about themselves over the years? And how many times have you gotten caught up in a story that has gone viral, only to find out it's not true? How many times did you see a picture you thought was real, only to find out it was photo-shopped after you have already passed it on to other people, or worse yet, all 874 of your "single-serving-friends" on Facebook? What about accidently sending a derogatory poison-pen e-mail or post to the wrong person? That "send" button can be a real bitch sometimes.

If people would stop posting comments about their meaningless lives, then maybe people would stop posting meaningless responses. But that very lifestyle and pop culture is what drives us as a society today. It's what's important. A "friend" recently posted a picture of her breakfast, which was a triple stack of pancakes with syrup running off the sides with a healthy topping of blueberries and whipped cream. The picture was accompanied by the post, "Another day in paradise!" The comments that followed were:

- Yum! Yum!

- OMG that looks so good!

- You lucky girl you!

- I wish I was there

- Save some for me;-)

Seriously people! This is what we live for? We constantly gripe and complain about not having enough hours in a day, but somehow we find time to log onto Facebook numerous times a day to read and post crap like this. If you have befriended Burger King on Facebook or follow McDonald's on Twitter, then you desperately need a life. Get a girlfriend, get a boyfriend, get a job, write a book, do something meaningful with your life. Get off your ass, go to the Internet addiction clinic, and get yourself a healthy dose of intervention because we are all becoming the home of the Whopper, both literally and figuratively!

Society a la Mode

Since I prefer life with a cherry on top, allow me to indulge you with a story of the crème de la crème that life has to offer.

Pulling into the Walmart parking lot, I was immediately confronted by another car coming head on in the opposite and wrong direction. The lane I was in was clearly marked with large white arrows spaced every hundred feet or so, all pointing in the same direction, which also happened to be the direction in which I was traveling. And if that wasn't enough to give away the fact that this was a one-way drive aisle, the forty-five-degree parking to my left and to my right all facing the same direction should have given someone who was halfway coherent, conscientious, or considerate the clues that they were headed in the wrong direction. Maybe they were oblivious, or maybe they just didn't give a shit. Either way, I was just happy that we squeezed by each other without taking off our side mirrors, and they drove past without stealing the parking spot I had been eyeing four spaces ahead.

I was only going there for deodorant, hotdog buns, and whatever candy bar looked good in the spur of the moment at the checkout line. I promised myself not to get distracted by the $5.99 video rack or any other falling prices that may hit me in the head. It was a ten minute or less in-and-out mission.

I squeezed out of my vehicle, trying not to hit the guy next to me, who so graciously parked over the yellow line, with my car door. I locked the doors and made my way to the monolith of a main entrance, which beckoned to me. I grabbed the first of many shopping carts strewn about the parking lot and escorted it into the facility like a cub scout escorting a little old lady across the street. There was a shopping cart corral two parking spaces up, but obviously most people only considered this a suggestion and would rather have their carts sweep across the parking lot and bang into a car bearing thirty-day tags, as many of those carts will do on breezy evenings such as that one.

I passed by an SUV—a forest green GMC Yukon to be exact. It had rolled into the closest handicap parking spot it could find, and all four doors opened up fast and furiously. There were no handicap tags on the back, but as I walked past, diverting my path slightly to avoid mowing over the barrage of way too excited ADHD children exiting the vehicle, I did notice a temporary handicap permit hanging from the rearview mirror. All the passengers, including the driver, were jovial and seemed to have no visible infirmities, except, perhaps, for the fact that they all seemed to have some sort of genetic eating disorder and could possibly be candidates for a new reality TV show called *The Enormous Loser.*

As I entered the grand façade and into the awaiting allure of excitement, my peripheral vision caught two individuals, one with an oxygen tank and tubes up his nose, and another "enormous loser," bickering over who would get the last available electric cart. "Stay focused," I reminded myself. "Ten minutes or less!"

I passed by Kay, my Walmart people greeter person of the moment, who simply smiled and said, "Good evening." It actually seemed somewhat genuine and unscripted as a warm fuzzy feeling swept over me. Whenever I patronize places like that, I typically am reminded of the Costco people greeter of the future from the movie *Idiocracy,* who stands at the door, emotionless and sedated, and repeats, "Welcome to Costco. I love you. Welcome to Costco. I love you."

The florescent lights mounted high above and chained to the white painted bar joists seemed brighter than necessary and dispersed an unexplainably odd color—a yellowish tint different from your average florescent. One could be made to believe, or at least I was made to believe in my justifiably paranoid ways, that these lights were scientifically designed to subdue the mind, like an external form of Prozac, radiating the body and subliminally forcing unsuspecting people to buy, buy, buy.

I was making a beeline to the hotdog buns when a gentleman came out of aisle six and walked in front of me, which gave me time to study his boxers. Now I've seen pants pulled down below someone's ass with his boxers pulled up to his waist, as this is the norm of today's low-budget fashion mix, but this guy was on the cusp of something big. A fashion revolution! He was wearing shorts, the waistline of which was pulled down to just above his knees, which caused him to walk like a woman in a long, tight dress. Taking petite, little-woman steps definitely did not jive with his badass, manly, upper body demeanor. Tucked into his shorts and rising up to the bottom of his ass was a pair of boxers, and tucked into those boxers and terminating at his waistline were another pair of boxers—a beautifully color coordinated, double-layered boxer ensemble. The only thing missing was a tweed peek-a-boo cardigan jacket and matching pompadour heels. You go, boy!

Just as I was beginning to ponder that fashion cataclysm way too much, I was cut off by a renegade electric cart pulling out of aisle thirteen, which forced me to a complete halt. The operator of the vehicle, without saying a word, made a feeble "thank you" hand gesture and kept on keepin' on.

Arriving at my first destination, I was distracted by the way too many choices of hotdog buns available to the consumer, and by a child standing in a shopping cart, violently shaking it and screaming bloody murder. His oblivious mother (oblivious, not in the traditional sense of the word, but oblivious in that she could not care less) went about her task of choosing the most appropriate pita chips for her weekend dinner party. I grabbed a pack of Mary Jane buns, and I was off to my next destination.

Backtracking through the deli meats section, I passed a man wearing a two-sizes-too-small wife-beater with plenty of exposed underarm hair and well-defined nipples, which segued right into the international Italian foods section where a pregnant woman wore a spaghetti strap top, with exposed navel and muffin top. It made me stop and think that I should have gotten hamburger buns instead.

Turning left, I traversed the store, passing by women's lingerie to my left and the shoe section to my right. A man and woman were both squatted down, looking at size-eleven sneakers on the bottom rack. The man-crack on him and exposed tramp stamp, with accompanying black thong, on her made me start humming "Ain't Too Proud to Beg" by the Temptations, and I wondered if the sneakers would actually be put to any productive use.

Continuing down the central corridor, men's fashions appeared on my left, electronics to my right, and right there in the middle of the corridor was the discount DVD display. "Don't look at it," I said to myself. "Keep moving! Stick to the mission!" A mom parked on the other side of the DVD display was checking them out. When her three-ish-year-old kid reached out from the confines of his car seat and grabbed a video, the mom smacked him on the hand and screamed, "Didn't I tell you not to touch nothing? How many times do I have to tell you to stop touching things?"

Better you than me, kid! I thought to myself. Maybe if we could "wife swap" with the mom over in the pita chip section, the kids might have a fighting chance. But of course, that will never happen.

Passing the DVDs, I could feel the tension begin to build in my brow. I glanced at my watch. Five minutes down, five to go. Stay focused. I made a left at home décor and was on the back-stretch to the pharmacy and bathroom departments when I was involved in another near miss with an electric cart. *They're like flies,* I thought to myself. *Quiet and pesky.*

Arriving at my final destination, it was difficult finding what I wanted. An unscented roll-on, any brand would do. *Is that too much to ask? Let's see, what's this flavor? Musk. No, that's not it. Wild Musk. No, not it either. Spice. No. Cool Metal. No.* A grown woman in my peripheral vision wearing SpongeBob pajamas and mismatched slippers, was scouring the feminine products area. I didn't even want to know. *Fuji, Fever, Game Day, Pure Sport, Ultimate Sport, Energy Surge, Pacific Surge, Denali, Silver Ion, Cool Impact, Arctic Edge, Ice, Voodoo, Conviction, Dark Temptation, Euphoria, Time Release Molecules. Fuck!!!*

I was standing in the express checkout lane, unsure how I got there. Transported in time, I suppose, by a momentary cerebral hemorrhage or some innate survival instinct that blocked out the last two minutes of my life. I only knew that I was there with my two measly items, fist clenched and adrenaline pumping, staring up at the sign that read "Twenty Items or Less." Since when did twenty items become an *express* line? I leaned to the side. There were five people in front of me. One of them had apparently had a freak accident in the sporting goods section and got her face caught in a fishing tackle box, and at least three of them hadn't passed first-grade math, or didn't care that they had a grocery cart full of items, or both. And the checkout girl certainly wasn't going to say anything for fear of getting sued or, at the very least, making a terrible scene for being so inconsiderate to the folks who couldn't care less about consideration in the first place. I glanced at my watch. Thirteen minutes. Three minutes over the limit. Fuck it! I grabbed two Snickers and a Twizzlers.

I smiled forcefully as I walked past the once lovely Kay, who now not only didn't seem to remember me, but looked at me with narrowed eyes of suspicion, which seemed to say, "What you got in that bag there, mister? Let me see your receipt!" Visions of the Wicked Witch of the West rushed past me as I chanted to myself, "There's no place like home. There's no place like home."

The automatic sliding door opened, and the fresh air of ninety-seven degrees, 100 percent humidity, and car exhaust fumes await-ed me. What a relief. I stopped at the forty-foot wide, white-paint striped, pedestrian crosswalk for a chance to make my getaway. Apparently, forty-feet isn't wide enough for most drivers to clearly see when they're traveling at five miles per hour, or maybe they just didn't care. Either way, it was a game of chicken, and only the luckiest and fastest would survive. One car drove by, then another, and then another. Should I stay or should I go now? One finally stops. All the windows are rolled up and tinted black. The bass is so loud, you can see the side mirrors vibrating with the music, or whatever you call it, with its bitch this and fuck that. Because of the window tint, I cannot see any occupants in the vehicle. Is someone waving me on? Are they having a seizure? Is this a man against the machine moment? I feel like an unwilling participant in Steven King's novel *Christine*. I chanced it, like a squirrel cross-ing a busy five-lane highway, and made it alive and unscathed to live another day.

My keys out, I unlocked my car door as a nearby car alarm started going off—a metaphor for my life! I don't even bother to look as most people wouldn't bother to either. I plopped down in the seat, took a deep breath, and looked at my watch. Twenty-seven minutes of my life gone, never to get back again. What else is new? Fuck it!

OK, so I have a confession to make. The story I just described didn't happen all in one trip to Walmart. But I am willing to bet my firstborn, Morgan, that given two, or perhaps no more than three, trips to Walmart (or Costco or Big Lots or Target or Sam's Club or Kmart or BJ's or Golden Corral or Piggly Wiggly) or a hundred other places for that matter, that I would experience the full realm of each and every one of these societal nightmares from which I will never awake, at least not in this lifetime.

There was a time when it mattered when people went into public to conduct their daily affairs. It was important to them and their family name, and it was a source of personal pride how one dressed and behaved in front of others. But the days of Georges Seurat's *Sunday Afternoon on the Island of La Grande-Jatte* are over. And I'm glad they are because I would hate to wear a bow tie and top hat to the beach while my woman bears a hoopskirt and umbrella. But given the choice between then and now, take me back to the past anytime.

Excuse me while I pull my britches up!

The Wrongness of Political Correctness

A friend of mine works for a government military contractor. He was sitting in a staff meeting one day with his fellow co-workers, his immediate boss, and his boss's boss, the department head. They were discussing concerns, or shall we say, challenges (you can't say problems anymore) in their department that resulted from the actions (you certainly can't say fuckups) of a supervisor who was relieved from his job responsibilities (God forbid we use the words "terminated" or "fired") because he was a "slacker." (Can I say that? Mr. ACLU, please don't take me to court, or boycott my book, or send henchmen to my house to perform dubious deeds. Please, I beg of you! I am but a starving writer who has enough problems with all the other assholes in my life. Can I say assholes?) At one point during the staff meeting, my friend piped up, and when referring to the guy that got fired (Fuck it. I said it!), he replied to his boss:

"Well, the problem was that he just didn't give a damn."

His boss shot a quick glance over to *his* boss, looked back at my friend, and replied, "You can't say that!"

"I can't say what?"

"You can't say that he didn't give a damn."

"Why not?"

"Because it's insensitive, demeaning, and against HR policy."

"But it's the truth."

"I don't care. It's inappropriate."

"So what am I supposed to say?"

"You can say he was…indifferent."

He's *indifferent*. Isn't that lovely? I have grandkids, and when they were about seven or eight, I told them a joke: What did the momma beaver say to the baby beaver? Shut the dam door! The grandkids rolled on the floor and thought it was damn funny. And now that we're adults, we can't use the word "damn?" Are we seven years old all over again?

Apparently the truth isn't important anymore, or at least it's not as important as how we package our verbiage. (As a disclaimer, I would like to point out that when I just used the word "package," I was using it as a verb, not a noun referring to my junk. So if any of you were offended, I make no apologies.) Political correctness is one of those societal disgraces that have risen from the ashes of the self-esteem movement and the societal philosophy that everyone has the right not to have their feelings hurt, regardless of the situation, the facts, or the truth!

Illegal immigrants aren't illegal anymore. They're simply undocumented workers. Mexicans are no longer Mexicans. They're Hispanic. Thanks to the media and politically correct advocates, we now have a new subclass of Mexicans (Pardon me. I mean Hispanics.) known as White Hispanics. Why aren't they Hispanic-Americans? I'm confused! You can't be homosexual anymore, but you can be a GLBTQ2IA (If you don't know what that is, I will let you look it up for yourselves.). Terrorist aren't terrorists anymore. They're something else, as not to provoke them.

There are some examples where I agree that names or titles should have been changed. I would like to think that those changes are made out of a societal evolution or a greater awareness of a particular situation, not just a feel-good, hypersensitive, politically correct overreaction of the moment, as they typically are. One example is that we stopped referring to individuals with certain disabilities as retarded and started using the term "disabled." I believe that was a move based on a greater understanding of institutionalized individuals that evolved over time. But then disabled was no good, and we had to say "intellectually challenged." But after a while, we had nothing better to do, so we deemed intellectually challenged inappropriate and had to start referring to them as "special needs." Is special needs really more evolved than intellectually challenged? In some ways, I think it's more demeaning. I know it's a sensitive subject, and we as a civilized society (moot, rhetorical, oxymoron) should be conscientious and sensitive to this fragile population. But at the rate we're going, pretty soon we'll be referring to individuals with disabilities as "empowered champions of adversity," or some other equally innocuous, feel-good-about-ourselves synonym or acronym of distinction that will do absolutely nothing to find a cure or further the cause. And lo and behold, it won't be long until even that term is considered offensive, and we will waste our precious resources seeking something of even higher consciousness that will make everything right with the world (as if we even know what higher consciousness means anymore). If we put as much energy into finding a cure as we do into debating and changing the name every decade or so, maybe we could eradicate the word or phrase altogether, or at the very least, only read about it in history books.

We no longer have problems to solve in this world of ours; we simply have challenges to overcome or tasks to complete. And in accomplishing those tasks, we never make mistakes anymore; we only have learning experiences to help us along the way. And if we have too many learning experiences, it's not because we're stupid or irresponsible; rather, it's because we're intellectually impaired.

And, of course, if we are intellectually impaired too many times, it doesn't matter in the grand scheme of things because we will never fail. We will just experience temporary deferred success. Some will argue in my defense that *my* deferred success in life has been a result of my intellectual impairment, which resulted from the learning experiences of numerous tasks in my youth, but I beg to differ. The fact of the matter is I failed because of my stupidity from not learning from my many mistakes along the way, and I will be the first to admit it in those terms!

The paragraph above gives but a few overly simplified examples of how this disease of political correctness has crept into every aspect of our lives, both professionally and personally. It is a disease that was borne out of the cultural revolution of the '60s and buried its roots on the heels of the self-esteem movement of the early '70s. From those humble beginnings, political correctness spread like wildfire into every crevice of society, and eventually proliferated into affirmative action, giving way to reverse discrimination, which, as we all know, has made everything right with the world.

If research scientists could spend their time, energy, and resources developing a prescription drug for PC instead of SAD, perhaps a smidgen of common sense could be restored to humanity.

I think General George S. Patton put it best when he said, "An army without profanity couldn't fight its way out of a piss-soaked paper bag!"[1] Tell it like it is, George! Oh, I'm sorry—tell it like it *was*, George! Tell it like it was!

Well Excuuuuuse Me!

*I*n the first chapter, I referenced Joe Queenan's book *Balsamic Dreams* regarding how the baby boomers were the beginning of the end for modern-day society. They started out with dreams to change the world, but in the end, they became nothing more than obnoxious sellouts who were only good at making money. One of Joe's contentions in his book is the overreaction to everything. This refers to the fact that no one can take a commonsense approach to anything and must overreact with hysteria to everything that goes on among us.

In 1980, I turned eighteen years of age. It was a long awaited milestone for your typical teenager because, at the time, eighteen was the legal drinking age (emphasis on the word "legal"). But there was also a social awakening going on concerning drinking and driving. Drunk driving was a joke, a slap on the wrist. No one took it seriously because if you got busted (assuming you didn't maim or kill anyone, and even then the consequences for your actions were pretty diluted compared to today), all you needed was a decent lawyer, and you got a modest fine, a good talking to by the judge, and you were free to become a repeat offender if you were so unlucky as to get caught again.

But as more and more innocent people got killed by drunk drivers, a powerful grassroots campaign arose, lobbying against the stupidity of driving while intoxicated and bringing the problem to the front pages and editorials of our nation's newspapers. With pressure mounting, lawmakers had two choices: 1) Address the seriousness of the situation by simply enforcing numerous laws already on the books and start holding people accountable for their actions or 2) Raise the legal drinking age to twenty-one. And I think we all know which simple, commonsense approach our esteemed elected lawmakers and politicians ended up taking.

But for me, being born and raised in the great state (commonwealth) of Virginia, my story had an even more convoluted twist to my martini. You see, when the decision came down the pike to raise the drinking age from eighteen to twenty-one, Virginia decided to do it in increments and did not make it retroactive for anyone who was already eighteen at the time. So here is my teenage, alcohol-induced dilemma:

- August 1980: I turned eighteen and was legal to drink alcohol.

- January 1981: The legal drinking age was raised to nineteen.

- January 1983: The legal drinking age was raised to twenty-one.

Therefore, I was legal to drink alcohol for four months—from August to December 1980. And then for eight months, from January to August 1981, it was illegal for me to drink alcohol. In late August 1981, it was once again legally OK for me to consume my PBR. Talk about adding insult to injury! Maybe I should have hired a personal injury attorney instead.

By losing the inability to come to some common sense understanding of problems (most of which *we* created) in this ever-changing world, we simply ignore them, kick the can down the proverbial road, and then overcompensate for our indiscretions by doing a complete one-eighty, which is equally disgraceful. But of course, with something as innate as common sense waning among us, it's no wonder we can't fix our most basic problems.

Here, for your reading pleasure, are but a few of the social overreactions we have faced in the past several decades:

- We couldn't enforce existing DUI and DWI laws that were already on the books, so we had to raise the drinking age to twenty-one. I know the old adage "Old enough to go to war, but not old enough to drink" is overused, but it's so ridiculous, and it's so true.

- Because of child abuse and unfit parents, no one can spank their kids or discipline them anymore. All we can do is put them in time-out (ugh, I mean their thinking chairs) for five minutes.

- We can't enforce existing gun laws and hold people accountable for their firearms, so we have to ban them altogether.

- We can't take the really decent health care system we have in this country and make it better, so we throw it out the window and start from scratch with the Affordable Care Act, which will be neither affordable nor health care when the dust settles.

- We can't fix our immigration problem, so we just give all the illegals amnesty. We are already rewriting the legal definition of the word "illegal" simply because it no longer suits our needs.

- Affirmative Action! We can't have an equal playing field and give everyone the same opportunities based on their own merits, so we go out and create a system that does just the opposite and causes reverse discrimination.

- Can't balance a budget? Let's just print more money, or borrow more money, or both, as we have done for decades, and see where that eventually takes us. Hello, Detroit! Hello, California! Hello, America! Hello, France, Greece, Italy, Spain, Germany, Ireland, England, Japan…

- On the one hand, we can't teach abstinence to kids in school today, but on the other hand, we can't teach birth control to teens either. I have a great idea! Why can't we do both? Why does it always have to be one or the other? Why can we no longer come together with a commonsense solution to our most basic societal dilemmas?

I could get carried away with hundreds upon hundreds of everyday overreaction stories happening all around the globe today, but instead, allow me to indulge in my most favorite:

The March 25, 2013 issue of the *Independent,* a British newspaper published in London, told a real-life story that reads like a fairy tale from hell. The title of the article is "*School in Essex Bans Triangle Shaped Flapjacks after Pupil is Hurt.*"[1] The essence of the story is there was a food fight in the school cafeteria. A flapjack (a pancake) that was cut into triangular-shaped pieces was thrown at another kid and hit him in the eye. The kid's eye became irritated, and he went to the hospital and was examined by a physician. Everything was fine, and the doc gave the kid some eye drops and sent him home. The commonsense thing to do would be to suspend the kid who started the food fight and put into place a progressive corrective action plan with more serious consequences if it happened again in the future. End of story, right? Wrong! That would make too much sense and, I'm sure, violate the kid's human rights in some way. So what intellectual decision does the school make concerning the matter? They ban triangular-shaped flapjacks and "have been told to cut flapjacks into rectangles or squares rather than triangles." The article continues by saying, "Critics have pointed out that a square flapjack has more sharp corners than a triangle shaped one." Now our educated school principals and superintendents are debating whether or not a flapjack with four corners is deadlier than a three-sided flapjack. Oh, don't get too snug because the article continues: "This is not the first time flapjacks have been banned for being a risk. Famously, Education Secretary Michael Gove was stopped from taking flapjacks—given to him by his wife—into a cabinet meeting in 2011. He was detained by security at the time and told the flapjacks were a security risk and would not be allowed in the cabinet room." Now pancakes can't even be trusted in the hands of adults and are considered a "security risk." Well excuuuuuse me!

We are losing our minds, ladies and gentlemen! And as if this story isn't pathetic enough, below is a response from a blogger who goes by the handle Elth N'Sayfty, which was posted immediately following the article:

> I would like to defend the stance taken by Castle View School...I have personally been responsible for implementing a wide variety of safety measures at schools in the Humberside area. For example, in the dining room I wanted to limit the

impact of biscuits being propelled across the room and now they are crushed into approx. 0.55 mm pieces, which reduces the force of a crushing blow to the head. In the classroom—rubbers [rubber bands] must be under 1 inch in diameter and rulers are limited to 5 cm—I negotiated a deal with a stationary company to get these custom made. Finally, in the playground—each kid is fitted with shoulder and knee pads together with a limit on the pace of running—no child is allowed to gallop into anything remotely approaching a jog. Results—no food, classroom, playground accidents reported in 1 year. So, I think you all need to step back here and just appreciate the measures this school takes to keep children safe. Well done, Castle School, well done.

For the love of humanity, someone please tell me this is a cynical and sarcastic response to the article! A joke! Someone please help me figure out what the unintended consequences of this overprotective spoilage might be! "Biscuits...crushed into approx. 0.55 mm pieces, which reduces the force of a crushing blow to the head." I can't even comprehend what the hell Elth N'Sayfty is talking about here! A crushing blow to the head—is he talking about biscuits or hammers? "...rubbers [rubber bands] must be under 1 inch in diameter and rulers are limited to 5cm." What the hell, let's go ahead and ban Lincoln Logs while we're at it. After all, they're about the same mass and weight as a wooden ruler. Why don't we leave the training wheels on our five-year-olds bike and never take them off? Hell, let's go ahead and ban bikes, scooters, skateboards, and motorcycles altogether! What about bunk beds and pillow fights? I don't know any family who owns a bunk bed that hasn't spent at least one night in the emergency room as a result of them. Let's ban gymnastics and boxing and wrestling and soccer and football and karate for kids! After all, aren't those potentially dangerous sports that routinely result in bruises, sprains, sutures, torn ACLs, torn rotator cuffs, and broken bones? And if "no child is allowed to gallop into anything remotely approaching a jog," then let's ban the one hundred-yard dash and all other track and field events to ensure that no one will ever injure themselves in any way, as this would be horrific. How about baseball with all her "ballistic projectiles," as ignorance would call them, being propelled at players and unsuspecting fans in attendance? Let's reduce the bat size to sixteen inches long and the baseball to a Ping-Pong-sized ball in an effort to mitigate the chances of injury from anyone getting hit in the head! America's pastime truly will be a...pastime! I've got another great idea. Why don't we just ban anything that moves, anything that can be picked up or thrown? When will we all become a boy in a bubble? Well done, Elth N'Sayfty! Well done!

Let me give another quick example of this overreaction insanity spreading through our culture like an out-of-control wildfire sparked by someone throwing his or her cigarette butt out the car window while driving through Yosemite on a smoldering August afternoon. There's a story about seven-year-old Josh Welch who got suspended from second grade because he chewed his Pop-Tart into the shape of a gun: "Josh Welch was suspended March 1 for two days after school officials accused him of shaping the pastry into the form of a gun and waving it around."[2] Have we lost our minds? If we really feel the need for some discipline here, can't we just send the kid to the principal's office, which is usually enough to make a second grader piss in his pants, and tell him, "Look kid, in this day and age, it's inappropriate to talk about guns or bring play guns to school, so just cool it and stop chewing your food into the shape of a gun, comprende?" No, we can't do that, can we? We have to go into hysteria mode and suspend the kid for two days.

Andres Serrano received international fame and recognition for his photo "Piss Christ," a photograph of a crucifix submerged in the artist's own urine, and we're going to suspend the Pop-Tart kid from elementary school? If he can chew his way through a Pop-Tart with such precision and talent that it is recognizable as a gun, don't suspend him, give him an A in art class.

It won't be long (it's already happening in certain municipalities) before we will ban little plastic army men, squirt guns, Nerf guns, and anything that has to do with cowboys and Indians or cops and robbers. And the whole cowboys and Indians thing is a double-edged sword because on one hand, you have the whole issue with cap guns and tomahawks and bows and arrows with the suction cups on the ends, but on the other hand, you have the whole politically correct "insensitivity" issue concerning the Redskins.

The problem with these random acts of stupidity is that they're not so random anymore. In fact, they're becoming quite common—the societal norm. And for the rest of us, well, I suppose we just don't know what we're talking about. I guess we're just two wild and *craaaaazy* guys!

Rugged Collectivism

A friend of mine, a twenty-one-year-old college student, sent me a text not too long ago after exiting one of his American history classes saying that his teacher told the class, "The idea of rugged individualism, where people pull themselves up by their own bootstraps, is nothing more than a myth." What pissed me off the most about that statement was that the teacher stated it, and taught it to the young, impressionable future of this world as fact. He called it a myth, as if it was something we read our children in nursery rhymes and fairy tales. He didn't start out by saying, "In my opinion, the idea of rugged individualism..." So the future leaders of this world are being indoctrinated with the ideology that people can't do a damn thing for themselves, and it takes Big Brother government, you know the one we have come to despise and distrust, to do it for us.

It's true that we need local, state, and federal government to provide certain things in order for us to keep humming along. We need a military to provide national defense. A National Guard helps provide support in times of great natural disaster or in times of civil disobedience. We need roads and highways in order to conduct commerce in an efficient and competitive way. We need a local police force to keep law and order. We need hospitals and paramedical services to provide emergency services. We even need a few laws to keep honest people honest and put away the psychos.

But to suggest that an individual can't do anything for him or herself is bullshit and does nothing but create a downward spiral of dependence that, once indoctrinated into a culture, is hard to get rid of. Of course, the side effect of this culture of dependence is an entitlement mentality, where one feels entitled to things that inherently, since the beginning of civilization, were things one worked for.

It would be one thing if government, particularly on a federal level, did something, anything, in an efficient, fiscally responsible way. Then I could see more people believing in, and placing faith in, their government. But that concept of fiscal responsibility is so far removed from our heads of state that the only light at the end of the fiscal tunnel is a freight train named financial collapse, and it's headed straight for us.

Medicare and Medicaid are in serious financial trouble, and our astute politicians can't seem to fix it, yet they want us to believe that nationalized health care will be cheaper and more efficient.

Social security is going broke. Congress has been kicking that can down Pennsylvania Avenue for decades, and when they finally do get around to dealing with it, it will be some gross, asinine, convoluted, overreaction solution that will undoubtedly cause more harm than good because it wasn't dealt with thirty or forty years earlier.

The post office can't compete with UPS or FedEx, and even after significant cuts over the past several years, the USPS is still a money pit. I will let a recent article from the *Huffington Post* speak for itself: "The Unites States Postal Service is hemorrhaging money—$25 million a day to be precise. That's one frank admission that was made Wednesday by Postmaster General Patrick R. Donahoe, who blamed the government for preventing the post office from adapting to technological changes in the business world."[1] Did you catch that? The postmaster general himself blamed the government for the problem, and who would know better than he?

In addition to this, we have all heard horror stories of civilian and military contractors charging $500 for screwdrivers or $1,200 for toilet seats, and I can assure you they didn't jiggle the handle or lift the seat.

According to our own precious government statistics, straight from the Office of Management and Budget, for the past fifty years, from 1962–2012, the US government has had a budget deficit forty-five out of those fifty years.[2] If any family or small business operated in this manner, they would have been shut down forty-eight years ago, and their assets would have been auctioned off, unless you're Ford, Chrysler, or GMC in which case the government will just loan you money it doesn't have. In order to do so, they will have to print the money before they lend it so that *they* go broke before you do. No, wait, they're already broke! (Don't try to make too much sense of it.) In the private sector, this would be called fraud, embezzlement, and counterfeiting, but for all the rugged collectivist out there, it's called progress. It's business as usual, and according to them, it's absolutely necessary.

As of July 2013, the US national debt was $16.7 trillion dollars and counting, and the daily interest on that debt is in the neighborhood of 1.2 billion dollars a day. Just to clarify: 1 billion dollars is 1 thousand million, and 1 trillion dollars is 1 thousand billion (not 1 hundred billion, as many people believe). Our inept government spends 1.2 billion dollars (one thousand two hundred million or, twelve hundred million dollars) *per day* just to pay the *interest* on our national debt of 16.7 trillion dollars (one trillion is one million, million). Therefore, to make sense of this, you could say the national debt is currently sixteen point seven million, million dollars, or, sixteen million, million, seven hundred million dollars.

So once again I ask that you tell me one reason why we should place our trust in a lie. If absolute power corrupts absolutely, and we all know it does, then why on earth would we want to give an already corrupt and inefficient entity more power? Not to mention the fact that your party or your guy is not going to be in office forever. So when you advocate this power while your guy is in office, and he uses it to promote his cause and your cause, it's somehow considered progress and change for the good of the country and mankind. But as soon as the other party takes over and uses this same power we have given them, suddenly it becomes a gross abject abuse of power. Doesn't anyone remember George W. Bush and the War Powers Resolution of 2001 and 2002?

In writing this, I am reminded of a quote from the former president of the United States, founder of the University of Virginia, author and signer of the Declaration of Independence, Thomas Jefferson, who once said, "A government big enough to give you everything you want, is a government big enough to take away everything you have."[3] Thomas Jefferson himself grew to have such a disdain for government, particularly the office of president, that he intentionally left "third president of the United States of America" off the epitaph on his tombstone at his final resting place at Monticello.

I bet Aron Lee Ralston is happy he missed the rugged individualism myth lecture. Aron was just your average dude who had a passion for the outdoors. One day in 2003, while canyoneering solo down a narrow crevasse in southeastern Utah, a large boulder fell and pinned his right arm against the canyon wall. Trapped for five days and near death, Aron, using the torque of his body weight against the bolder, intentionally broke his radius and ulna bones in his right forearm, applied a tourniquet, and then self-amputated his arm. After doing so, he rappelled down the remaining sixty-five-foot sheer wall single-handedly and began to hike out of the canyon when he came across other hikers who called for help.[4]

The rugged collectivists out there would have you believe that Aron would be a skeleton hanging on a canyon wall had it not been for the Detroit automakers who made the car that the rescuers used to drive into the remote area where Aron was found. The same automakers were the recipients of subsequent government bailouts so they could continue making cars that save people's lives. The rugged collectivists will remind us that Aron would be a skeleton hanging from the canyon wall if it were not for the park rangers, employed by our government that built the roads into the park, paid for by taxpayer money, which allowed the rescuers to get to Aron; or the cell phone subsidies our government hands out to low income individuals; the FCC who controls and monitors the airways; the permits that the government hands out to build the cell phone towers; or, all other infrastructure that the government provided so that the company that made the knife that Aron used to amputate his own arm could prosper.

Yes, the rugged collectivists out there will insist that if it were not for all these, Aron would have died out there in the canyon. But I beg to differ. Being a holdout and one of a handful of believers in the human spirit and the ideology of rugged individualism, I believe Aron would be a skeleton hanging from the canyon wall if it were not for, Aron.

Thank you, Aron, for showing us that true grit and rugged individualism, although waning and perhaps on life support in today's society, *is* still alive in the indomitable human spirit.

It's a very, very dangerous turning point when people no longer believe in themselves and start turning to Big Brother government for all the answers and all the entitlements. They turn to the same government that they have come to distrust and despise to the point that a majority of us don't even vote, and yet we believe that we can't make it without them. Perhaps we should pause and ask ourselves, "What is a government?" or, more appropriately, "What is it that comprises a government or any other entity for that matter?" It is a plurality of us—individuals, we the people! And that is where the creativity and ingenuity starts—with *us*. So if we stop believing in ourselves and start to believe that things can only be accomplished with the help and blessing of the grossly bloated and horribly inefficient political and governmental complex, then it appears *we* have just created the greatest oxymoron of all time!

> Nothing in the world can take the place of persistence. Talent will not; nothing is more common than unsuccessful men with talent. Genius will not; unrewarded genius is almost a proverb. Education will not; the world is full of educated derelicts. Persistence and determination alone are omnipotent. The slogan, 'Press On!' has solved and always will solve the problems of the human race.[5]
>
> —Former president of the United States, Calvin Coolidge

The Persnickety Nihilist

Persnickety:
1. Obsessed with detail—overly attentive to detail and trivia, (informal); **2. Snobbish**—United States snobbish in terms of choice, and thus wanting or accepting only the finest things; **3. Requiring keen eye for detail**—United States necessitating precise, keen attention to detail.[1]

Nihilist:
nihilism (noun) 1. Total rejection of social mores—the general rejection of established social conventions and beliefs, especially of morality and religion; **2. Belief that nothing is worthwhile**—a belief that life is pointless and human values are worthless; **3. Disbelief in objective truth**—the belief that there is no objective basis for truth.[1]

*O*nce upon a time, not too terribly long ago, our great, great-grandfathers had to sharpen their axes, harness up the horse and wagon, go out and chop down a tree, hack all the branches off of it, saw the trunk into two-foot sections, quarter each section, load all the tree parts into the wagon, haul it a quarter mile to the house, neatly stack all the firewood in close proximity to the cabin, haul a smaller stack of twenty or so pieces into the cabin, properly stack three or four of those pieces in the fireplace, light the fire with a match and sufficient kindling, and make sure he had enough to keep the fire stoked all winter long—a process that pretty much took all day and had to be repeated every month or so. (Today if the gas logs don't fire up after the third or fourth click of the remote, we start cussing and calling it a piece of crap.) All the while, Ma was down by the river, hand washing the clothes and the shit out of the baby's cloth diapers, and then brought them back to the cabin to hang up and air dry. No rest for the weary, she went straight to cutting the head off dinner, plucking it, quartering it, stoking the fire, and cooking it up. (Today if the free sample of Boar's Head pastrami at the deli counter doesn't taste fresh to our liking, we complain to the manager and head off to aisle six to buy our disposable diapers.)

The persnickety nihilist (PN) is a creature that wants it all, but doesn't want to do anything to get it. They gobble down their cake as fast as they can shove it into their throats, and they keep coming back for more. And the more they get, the more they want, and the more particular, snooty, and obnoxious they become.

If you walk into many fast-food franchises these days, the latest, greatest Coca-Cola self-serve dispenser boasts 120 different drinks to choose from. We don't need that many choices. We don't need half that many choices. But the persnickety nihilists will tell you they do, and how great it is, even though a majority of them will settle for their usual Diet Coke to offset their 1,800 calorie meal loaded with saturated fats.

We don't need 500 satellite TV channels. We don't need 200 cable TV channels. We don't need 100 TV channels. But the persnickety nihilists will tell you they take comfort in having all those channels, even though they routinely watch the same ten to twenty channels night after night.

The PN buys 2.7 million copies of the *Guinness Book of World Records* every year.[2] A book that was once a perfectly decent reference guide or interesting literary entertainment has turned into a prodigious personification of the persnickety nihilist, professing such monumental mankind achievements as, the longest distance skateboarding by a goat, largest display of origami boats, longest paperclip chain made in thirty seconds, the most Post-it notes stuck to a body, couple with the most body modifications, longest basketball spin on a toothbrush, heaviest weight lifted by eye sockets, and man with the "stretchiest" face. I don't think I will be seeing any of those amazing achievements on a job résumé anytime soon, unless you happen to be applying at Barnum & Bailey.

Segueing off the pretentiousness of today's *Guinness Book of World Records,* the PN has made a dais of recognition to everything and anything mundane, professing national days of recognition, such as, Gumbo Day, Free Thought Day, Sausage Pizza Day, Toilet Tank Repair Month (We're all going down the toilet.), Bring Your Teddy Bear To Work/School Day, Wiggle Your Toes Day, Lost Sock Memorial Day (Personally, I despise the fact that this is referred to as a memorial day.), Pecan Month (A whole month, wow!), Walk Around Things Day (Don't know or even care what this is.), Costume Swap Day (?), Squirrel Awareness Month (Different than Squirrel Appreciation Day in January.), Carry A Tune Week, World Menopause Day (I'm sleeping in on that one.), and Survivors of Suicide Day (Forgive me if I'm being insensitive, but do suicide survivors really need a day to be reminded why they were calling it quits? I think reading this chapter would be more than adequate to jog their memory). There is also Bring Your Daughter to Work Day. Does that apply to prostitutes? These are just a few of the literally thousands upon thousands of mundane national days, weeks, and months,[3] of recognition created out of a sense of need and importance by none other than the persnickety nihilist. Maybe if we took the National Day of Reason (typically celebrated in May) and National Use Your Common Sense Day (typically celebrated in November), and turned each of them into a month of remembrance instead of a day, we could, as a species, start evolving again.

The PN will have an oblique opinion about everything political, even though they never vote.

The PN will bitch and complain about environmental issues and act like they're out to save the world, yet the only thing most of them do is recycle their plastic bottles and aluminum cans, and screw newfangled corkscrew light bulbs into their lamps. Ed Bagley Jr. is a man I could have an intelligent conversation with. Why? Because as a devout environmentalist, he puts his money where his mouth is. He is a man who practices what he preaches, a man who leads by example, and a man of principle in terms of his environmental beliefs. There are not many like him out there these days.

The persnickety one will gripe about human rights issues in the United States of America, and the nihilist in them will turn right around and buy their T-shirts, underwear, dress shirts, slacks, coffee, wine, and every other commodity from China, Venezuela, Burma, Ethiopia, Pakistan, India, Bangladesh, Vietnam, Columbia, Nicaragua, or Indonesia without giving it a second thought.

The PN can't stop complaining about evil corporate America and then turn around and load up their 401K with evil corporate America.

The PN make themselves feel better by embracing political correctness. Sorry Ms. Paltrow, you're not consciously uncoupling, you're getting a divorce. Deal with it!

The PN will blame their parents for everything that's gone wrong in their lives and take personal credit for anything positive, while their own heinous offspring run around at their feet, spoiling the party for everyone. Yes, the persnickety nihilists will go to their graves believing their parents had it all wrong and were stupid and ignorant. But oh, how *they* are doing such a far superior job raising *their* kids with their ADD, and their ADHD, and their spoiled behavioral issues, and their obesity, and their food allergies, and their inhalers, and their medical issues, and their prescription drugs.

The PN believe, by virtue of their own benevolence, that they are above the rest of us, just like all the pop stars, movie stars, and politicians who get busted for DUI and expect to get out of it just because of who they are. These stars are multimillionaires but they can't be bothered to have a designated driver or hire a limo to take them clubbing or dining or whoring. Or how about the likes of people like Michael Vick who had it all, so he had to go out and organize something so juvenile and primeval as a dog fighting ring just to keep himself entertained? How about our beloved O. J. who, after getting away with murder, literally, just *had* to get his football cards back? Or Lindsay Lohan and all the other privileged folks out there who have it all, then turn around and piss it all away. Yes, it's the good old Richard Pryor, set yourself on fire while freebasing cocaine in a drug-and-alcohol-induced psychosis, phenomenon. This is the one popularized by Elvis, Joplin, Hendrix, and Morrison, and proudly carried on by the likes of Belushi, Chris Farley, Heath Ledger, Cory Monteith, River Phoenix, Whitney Houston, Grasshopper, the King of Pop, Philip Seymour Hoffman, and all the other thousands upon thousands of revolving door, Betty Ford Clinic participants. All the money and fame and everything else you ever dreamed of and wished for just isn't good enough to keep us happy anymore, is it?

All the comforts and conveniences we enjoy today aren't good enough for persnickety nihilists. The things in life that are important to them are all about style, comfort, and image. The PN will look you in the eye and tell you that the single most important thing in their lives is family, even though they are currently cheating on their spouses. They will tell you that the material things are not important in life, all while justifying the purchase of their new SUV which they can't afford, by spewing off that, according to consumer reports, it has the smallest carbon footprint of all the SUVs on the market. The persnickety nihilists will tell you that culture is important to them and the upbringing of their children, even though the only culture anyone in the family gets on a daily basis is three hours of reality TV and video games.

No matter how much they have or what they have achieved in this world, the PN are never satisfied, but they will tell you they are. The bottom line is the persnickety nihilists don't care about anyone but themselves. Society is being reduced to the "me" generation, or, perhaps more appropriately, the "look at me" generation.

Persnickety Nihilist: 1. One who is overly obsessed with him or herself. **2.** Overly attentive only to things that are important to oneself. **3.** One who thinks the world revolves around him or her. **4.** One who is never satisfied. **5.** Superficial. **6.** Pretentious. **7.** The next evolution of Homo sapiens.[4]

Hypocrites-R-Us

*T*he persnickety nihilist is a hypocrite. The rugged collectivist is a hypocrite. The racist is a hypocrite. Most politicians are hypocrites. Anyone who believes in higher taxes but has cheated on their income tax returns is a hypocrite. Anyone who professes strong family values while cheating on their spouse is a hypocrite. Anyone who procreates and abandons the responsibility of their actions is a hypocrite. Anyone who takes corporate or government bonuses while their corporation or government is going down the financial shithole is a hypocrite. Anyone who takes advantage of entitlements of any kind when they are more than able to contribute in one degree or another is a hypocrite. Anyone who professes to be a devout environmentalist and turns around and throws their cigarette butt out of their car window is a hypocrite. The backseat driver who happens to be a horrible driver is an unknowing hypocrite. Political correctness is a hypocrite. The out-to-save-the-planet person who brings his or her own reusable bags to the grocery store, then turns around and leaves his or her shopping cart in the middle of the parking lot instead of pushing it thirty feet to the nearest corral is probably a hypocrite and definitely an asshole. Anyone who routinely takes up two parking spaces, then complains about people taking up two parking spaces is *definitely* an asshole *and* a hypocrite. Anyone who says one thing but does another is a hypocrite. Anyone who does not lead by example is a hypocrite. The modern-day Homo sapien is a hypocrite! Have I covered everybody?

About forty years ago, Pink Floyd wrote the song "Money" in which they professed, "Money is the root of all evil today." I would agree with that if it wasn't for hypocrisy. I believe it goes deeper than that, and that money (greed) is but one of the many detrimental societal by-products that begins with hypocrisy. This hypocrisy has rooted itself so deeply within us and within our culture that it is now the norm of society, and no one really expects otherwise.

Hypocrisy is nothing more than being intellectually dishonest with oneself; a lie that we know to be true but it's OK because it's *our* dirty little secret. We look in the mirror and put on the face of integrity, but deep inside we know it's a lie. It's easier that way. It's easier to be disingenuous with ourselves than it is to be honest with ourselves. After all, being honest with ourselves requires integrity, principles, and, ah, honesty. If we can't be honest with ourselves, what are the chances we will be honest with anyone else in our personal, professional, or daily lives?

The fallout of this societal pestilence, this rampant, uncontrollable hypocrisy, is a society that has continued to rust from the inside out. This corrosion clouds people's judgment to the point where the ends are always justified by the means. People compromise their principles. People become blind to the truth to the point where they can't even recognize what the truth is anymore. And many of these people are in positions of power, both corporately and in government, and make decisions that will impact the future of the entire world. If that doesn't scare the hell out of you, then you're asleep at the wheel, or you're one of them, or probably both.

Failing to look at the picture objectively or from different perspectives is what hypocrites do best. We simply withdraw inside ourselves to protect the power, or perceived power, we have. And at the rate we are going, a hundred years from now our great, great,

great-grandchildren will be arguing over the same issues in the same fashion as we do today because none of us have the ability to look at things objectively or admit that there are consequences, unintended or otherwise, to our decisions and actions. They're always right and their opinion is gospel without any ramifications whatsoever. The more things change, the more they stay the same, now don't they?

In the meantime, let's just keep it to ourselves, this dirty little secret of ours. Don't rock the boat. Keep it in the family. Maintain the status quo. Life is good. Shhh!

Principles?

I love Chinese food, but I'm not a big fortune cookie fan and will usually pass on them, though not because I don't like them. In fact, I love to crumble them up and sprinkle them over my red bean ice cream after finishing my egg foo young. It's more a matter of principle for me. It's what's inside the cookie that matters to me. You see, back in the day, the essence of the cookie, the whole point of it, was to break it open and read your fortune, which was usually something meaningful and poignant, like a Confucian or Buddhist quote, such as "If you chase two rabbits, both will get away" or "There is no way to happiness. Happiness is the way." These were deep and meaningful passages that *meant* something, passages that got us to think outside our little insignificant world. But nowadays, for the most part, fortune cookie fortunes have descended into a muddle of tacky and superficial phrases, quotes, and anecdotes that are supposed to make us feel good about ourselves, such as "You have a bright and humorous personality." I doubt it. "Hard work will get you everything." Please!

The last meaningful fortune I got from a cookie is now matted and framed and hanging on the wall of my home office. It is a tiny white piece of paper centered in the middle of a large black-matted background, and reads, "It is easier to fight for your principles than to live up to them." People like to boast about their principles, about right from wrong, but when it comes to putting their money where their mouths are, few will actually pony up and live up to their own self-imposed expectations.

In 1989, when I was twenty-seven years old, I was watching the news on TV and saw a man holding a bag of groceries in each hand. (Actually I don't know what he had in each bag, but I like to think he was strolling home from the street market.) He was standing in front of a tank in Tiananmen Square. The tank stopped, and then tried to move to the man's left. The man stepped to the left. The tank tried to move to the man's right. The man stepped to the right. It was an honest-to-goodness Mexican standoff. He was a man of principle, a man with really, really big balls. He was there because of what he believed in, and those beliefs were being challenged and put down by a repressive government that believed *it* was better than the people it served.

In the time since that image became permanently etched in my mind, the instances of such integrity and principle have been few and far between. People like to talk a big game, but few actually step forward and do something about it.

Mother Theresa was a woman of principle, and she wore it on her sleeve like a badge of courage. She lived her mission and her principles day in and day out.

Jim Bakker was not a man of principle for all the obvious reasons. And now that I think about it, neither was Jim Jones, Jimmy Swaggart, Ted Haggard, Robert Tilton, David Koresh, Todd Bentley, Jason Russell, Eddie Long, all the priests who participated in the child sexual abuse scandal, all the priests who covered it up, and all the other scumbags out there who continue to abuse religion for their own personal gain. The spiritual list of perpetrators goes on!

What about the business world? Ever heard of Kenneth Lay or Bernie Madoff? Of course you have! Ever heard of Aaron Feuerstein? Most of us haven't because in the cliché world, good guys finish last. Good guys finish last because there are so few of them comingled among the crooks that when we do hear a blip about someone doing something extraordinarily good in this world it is overshadowed by the garbage and dirty laundry being broadcast over and over again on a host of twenty-four-hour news channels. Like a bad car wreck, we can't seem to get enough.

Aaron Feuerstein was the third-generation owner and CEO of Malden Mills in Lawrence, Massachusetts. A devastating fire during the night of December 11, 1995 burned the aging factory to the ground. Malden Mills was a privately held company, and the primary stakeholders were Aaron and his family. Most smart CEOs would have seized the opportunity to cash in on the lucrative insurance money or relocate the operations to another country, like everyone else; somewhere where child labor laws, unions, environmental restrictions, and minimum wage laws were minimal or nonexistent. But Aaron had more integrity than that. Not only did he decide to rebuild the factory right where it once stood, he kept the idle workers on payroll during the entire rebuilding process. He said, "I have a responsibility to the worker, both blue-collar and white-collar. I have an equal responsibility to the community. It would have been unconscionable to put 3,000 people on the streets and deliver a death blow to the cities of Lawrence and Methuen."[1] I can't really envision, nor do I ever remember, hearing a comment like that from mainstream corporate America—ever!

By contrast, people like Kenneth Lay, Jeffrey Skilling, Bernie Madoff, Barry Minkow, Joe Nacchio, Ramalinga Raju, Gregory Reyes, John Rigas, Bernard Ebbers, Calisto Tanzi, David Walsh, Dennis Kozlowski, Andrew Fastow, and Governor Rod Blagojevich seem to set the corporate standards of conduct for modern-day business ethics. (Even though Governor Rod probably belongs more appropriately in the *political* category as opposed to the *business* category, I stuck his name in here. After all, business corruption and political corruption seem to make the best bedfellows, don't they?) In stark contrast to Mr. Feuerstein, the standard operating procedures of these men seems to be fraud, money laundering, kickbacks, grand larceny, insider trading, lying to investors, encouraging investors to buy more company stock as they unload theirs, unethical accounting practices, misappropriating funds, etc.

Opponents of Mr. Feuerstein say he was financially irresponsible for paying his idle workers while the plant was being rebuilt and that this financial indiscretion forced Malden Mills to file for bankruptcy in 2001, resulting in Aaron being relieved of his CEO position by creditors. Coming to Mr. Feuerstein's defense, if it is true that the actions of paying those idle workers while the factory was being rebuilt caused Malden Mills to go bankrupt six years later, then why did Malden Mills, under new leadership and with a new CEO at the helm, again file for bankruptcy and close its doors for good in January 2007, six years after the first bankruptcy?[2] There will always be those whose ends justify the means with a dollar sign.

Abraham Lincoln was a man of principle (I had to go way back to come up with someone in the political arena). He didn't earn the nickname "Honest Abe" for nothing. He stuck by his principles in an unpopular war, and an even greater detested amendment, that tore the United States apart and, ultimately, cost him his life.

For every Abraham Lincoln, there are countless disingenuous people in politics who care more about achieving and maintaining power than they do about right from wrong, their constituents, or their country as a whole. Instead of boring you with a list of top contenders, allow me to cut to the chase and give you the Homo sapien at the top of my list—Marion Barry. If you don't know who he is, here are my CliffsNotes:

1979: Marion Barry is elected mayor of our nation's prestigious capital.

1983: Marion Barry is reelected mayor of our nation's prestigious capital.

1987: Marion Barry is again reelected mayor of our nation's prestigious capital.

1990: Marion Barry is caught red-handed in an FBI sting operation for cocaine possession and soliciting prostitution. "Bitch set me up" became his rallying cry.

1992: Marion Barry is released from federal prison after serving his time.

1993: Marion Barry runs for and is reelected mayor of our nation's prestigious capital.

In case you missed that last bit of information, allow me to reiterate—Marion Barry runs for and is *reelected* mayor of Washington, DC, our nation's prestigious capital.

It seems that Marion is a product of his society, one that tolerates and justifies any behavior for its own good. It's hard to tell who's really at fault—Marion or society. Is there really any difference between the two? Don't answer that. It was rhetorical!

Bill Clinton, during the whole Monica Lewinski affair, was not a man of principle. But it wasn't Bill's actions, as deplorable as they were, that bothered me so much, as I would not expect anything different from most other modern-day politicians. What deeply troubled me was the response by an overwhelming majority of his supporters, individuals and media alike, in the weeks and months that followed. During that time, few Clinton supporters said, "You know, Bill, you're our guy and we love you, but you screwed up and there needs to be some consequences for your actions." No, they justified his actions. "It's his personal life, and it's none of our business" was the basis for their defense. They even defended his lying to the American people by saying that it was a personal issue, it didn't pertain to his job, it didn't involve the American people, and thus we shouldn't be involved. No one seemed to care about the principle of the matter, although a few folks were on the fence about the whole affair but just couldn't seem to let their principles get in the way of their love for the guy.

Principles and integrity seem to be a thing of the past—some old-fashioned, retro concept that is still revered and preached only by aging grandfathers and great-grandfathers who don't even know how to operate a smartphone. Mohandas Karamchand Gandhi once said, "The roots of violence: Wealth without work, Pleasure without conscience, Knowledge without character, Commerce without morality, Science without humanity, Worship without sacrifice, Politics without principles."[3]

Come on, Gandhi, get with the times, Gramps! Get with the times!!

And All the Christians
Say Amen

S everal months ago, I was sitting at my favorite local dive, eating lunch and thumbing through the local paper. The headlines were the same depressing crap as the day before and most of the days before that, so I turned to the classifieds section to see what might pique my interest. I stumbled across a section that I had come across before but had long since tried to put out of my mind. Among the flea markets, garage sales, estate sales, pet stud services, foreclosures, and collectables, there it was, like the Holy Grail, sandwiched between the "found" and "travel vacations" sections (which I found insanely humorous and ironic)—religious announcements.

Using some common sense, one would think that this section would be cluttered with fundraisers that a local church was having on Saturday. But no, those announcements belong in the fundraisers section. Perhaps one would expect to find a listing of single mother support groups or Lamaze birthing classes, but no, those belong in the generic announcements section. It appears that this quite popular religious announcements section is reserved almost exclusively for personal "thank-yous" to none other than Saint Jude, the patron saint of hopelessness and despair. Based on the popularity of this section, I'm sure the next logical evolution of this particular medium will be to create a new St. Jude section exclusively for the man himself.

There were seven ads in this section on that particular day, and five of them, almost identical, read like this:

ST. JUDE NOVENA—Thank you, St. Jude, for prayers answered. May the sacred heart of Jesus be adored, glorified, loved, and preserved throughout the world now and forever. Sacred heart of Jesus, pray for me. St. Jude, Worker of Miracles, pray for me. St. Jude, Hope of the Hopeless, pray for me. Say 9 times a day for 9 days. Must promise publication. JK

I'm assuming that St. Jude's batteries in his hearing aid have long gone bad, so JK feels the burning desire to publish his personal message instead of kneeling, clasping his hands, and just talking directly to the man himself like most people have done for thousands of years. And what's up with the initials, JK? Do you think St. Jude would not be able to distinguish *your* classified ad from the other five almost identical ads (four of them identical except for the initials at the end of the message) without your initials at the end? If this is the case and St. Jude needed those initials for clarification, how would he decipher that they were *your* initials and not the initials of countless JKs in your immediate geographical region? I see this as a problem, JK. You wouldn't want another JK getting the credit and elevated spiritual status, now would you? One final note, JK, before you pass on advice, such as "Must promise publication," to other wannabe modern-day spiritual seekers, you should work through some of the questions I have posed here so that you don't get accused of fraud. You wouldn't want the ACLU breathing down your neck, would you?

I think one could make the case that the idea or concept of God began when our ancestor, Homo erectus, first learned to make controlled fire. Think about it—man now had the ability to create this magical, mysterious thing that he could not explain nor comprehend. It was a thing that brought great joy (It kept you warm during the Ice Age; you learned that a medium-rare woolly mammoth tasted so much better than a raw one; or you kept predators and ex-cavewomen at bay with this new magic at the end of a torch.) and, at the same time, could bring great pain, as many cavemen and Joan of Arc found out in years to come.

Since then, the idea or concept of God has become *the* most powerful force in human nature. Because of this, more and more innocent people have been murdered in the name of God than anything else. The Jews and Palestinians have been at each other's throats for longer than anyone can remember. The Crusades of eight hundred years ago slaughtered hundreds of thousands throughout Europe and Asia Minor. The whole purist race and divine race propaganda promulgated by the Nazis and the Nips ended up killing 60 million people in World War II. The ethnic cleansing that took place during the Bosnian war twenty years ago killed hundreds of thousands of innocent women and children. The jihad that is being waged today. Catholics vs Protestants. Sunni vs Shia. I could go on and on. Not to mention scandals of various kinds woven through the historical vestments of religion, some of which are too recent, too hideous, and too exposed to forget anytime soon. And every one of these people believes, truly believes, that they are looked upon with great esteem in God's eyes and that they are doing God's will.

Back in the Middle Ages, if you studied science and questioned whether the earth was, in fact, the center of the universe, as was the conventional and religious belief of the day, and openly spoke out that science was leaning toward the belief that *we* revolved around our sun and not vice versa, Christianity would have crucified you just for asking (now there's a kind and loving religion for ya). There have been numerous other times where religions have done a one-eighty and changed their stance on moral issues over the millennium. Does this mean that you're OK in God's eyes if you believe in what your church believes at the time it believes it? In other words, if your religion suddenly changes its mind because science has finally convinced it otherwise, and you change your mind and follow the teachings of your church at the moment the church says so (not a moment too soon or too late), then everything is kosher between you and God; but if your timing isn't on cue with that of your church, then you are a heretic worthy of being burned at the stake? Please! There's a reason why we're known as "mortal."

Comedian Emo Philips hit the crucifixion nail on the head when, in one of his most notorious stand-up routines, he said:

Once I saw this guy on a bridge about to jump. I said, "Don't do it!"

He said, "Nobody loves me."

I said, "God loves you. Do you believe in God?"

He said, "Yes."

I said, "Are you a Christian or a Jew?"

He said, "A Christian."

I said, "Me too! Protestant or Catholic?"

He said, "Protestant."

I said, "Me too! What franchise?"

He said, "Baptist."

I said, "Me too! Northern Baptist or Southern Baptist?"

He said, "Northern Baptist."

I said, "Me too! Northern Conservative Baptist or Northern Liberal Baptist?"

He said, "Northern Conservative Baptist."

I said, "Me too! Northern Conservative Baptist Great Lakes Region or Northern Conservative Baptist Eastern Region?"

He said, "Northern Conservative Baptist Great Lakes Region."

I said, "Me too! Northern Conservative Baptist Great Lakes Region Council of 1879 or Northern Conservative Baptist Great Lakes Region Council of 1912?"

He said, "Northern Conservative Baptist Great Lakes Region Council of 1912."

I said, "Die, heretic!" and pushed him over.[1]

Thank you, Emo, for that hilariously poignant yet sadly realistic analogy of what God means to us today.

It's no wonder more and more people are running away from the traditional religions and becoming atheists, or worse yet, joining some TV evangelist group. Have you seen the number of TV evangelists on the air these days and the number of people in attendance? Tens of thousands of people fill stadiums like it's the Jets versus the Colts in Super Bowl III, listening to these modern-day profits (excuse me, I mean prophets) scream and yell and hack up hair balls, wearing their gold jewelry and their designer clothes with their meticulously manicured hair, their mansions, and SUVs. Not to mention the millions upon millions of people watching on TV, drawn to this like moths to a flame. I can't think of one modern-day evangelist (certainly not one of the more popular and notorious ones) who is not insanely rich, not afraid or even slightly humbled to admit it, and worse yet, not afraid to put their wealth on display, all while interpreting the Bible in their own way that benefits and promotes an agenda that serves their needs and their bank accounts. Can I get a hallelujah?

Then there is a lovely Sunday drive out into the country to see all the prefabricated, metal-building churches, popping up on every forty acres with their witty marquees, enticing nonbelievers or believers looking to make a switch with prophecies like "Life Stinks? We Have A Pew For You"; "Alcoholics Welcome—Every Sunday We Turn Water Into Wine"; "Free Coffee, Everlasting Life.

Yes, Membership Has Its Privileges"; "Happy Hour Here Every Sunday"; "Prayer—Wireless Access To God With No Roaming Fee"; "Let's Meet at My House Sunday Before The Game—God"; "You Give God the Credit, Now Give God the Cash"; and "Don't Make Me Come Down There—God."

Or what about the Jehovah's Witnesses, the Hare Krishna's, and the host of other barnyard local religious groups banging on our doors and trying to solicit our souls with their contemporary spiritual advertising and recruiting efforts.

If this is the alternative to traditional religion, then it's pretty obvious why people are joining the atheists' faith. It's scary how many people flock to these types of spiritual connections, like a modern-day gold rush. This is a business-minded, artificial exploitation of God. But who can truly blame them? Everything else in our lives is artificial. Religion has become just another extension of that synthetic quality and a testament to who we are. It has little or nothing to do with God anymore, or compassion for our fellow man, but has everything to do with money, power, and killing and eradicating those who don't believe in the same profit, excuse me, prophet, that we do.

We can spend our entire lives truly believing in and worshiping God the way our religion has taught us. But the fact of the matter is, until we're dead, we won't know who's right and who's wrong, so let's stop acting like we have all the answers and we're better than everyone else. If the Jews are right in how they worship God, does that mean everyone else is going to hell? If Catholicism is right, are the rest of us screwed, regardless of how we have conducted ourselves in this world?

In a futile effort to unite all religions around the world, I would like to offer a simple and peaceful solution for all: religion should be reduced to one rule, one law of nature, one commandment—Love your neighbor as yourself. If that's too heavy for some of you

out there, here's a diluted version so as not to offend anyone—
One should treat others as one would like to be treated. After all,
isn't that what God and spirituality are all about? Don't answer
that, it was, well, you know, rhetorical.

And all the Christians say amen.

Uncommon Sense

S ince the beginning of time, every species that has ever lived has had within them an innate understanding of survival and the world around them. As described in the introduction of this book, even an amoeba, a brainless, single-cell organism and the most basic of all living things, has the intelligence to shy away from danger in its environment. So why is it that we, Homo sapiens, with all of our technology and monumental achievements, seem to be losing any and all rationale that is remotely equated with common sense?

We know that imagination levels in children have been on a consistent decline since the early 1990s. We know that IQ levels continue to decline in the developed world year after year, and we have a whole host of TV shows, like *Americas Dumbest Criminals, 1000 Ways To Die, The Darwin Awards,* and *Are You Smarter Than A Fifth Grader,* to not only prove it, but to flaunt it as if it's something to brag about.

This loss of rationale that mankind has perpetuated upon itself is the great felony of our time. But the even greater crime worthy of execution which may, in fact, be our own self-fulfilling prophecy, is that we are sitting around allowing it to happen. And not only are we doing nothing to correct this humanistic error of our ways, but we're contributing to it on a daily basis. It is the consequence, either unintended or a careful calculation, of everything among us, and not only do we stand by and watch it happen, we allow it to get progressively worse.

Eight years ago, around 2005, a friend of mine went to a remote part of South America with the Peace Corps for two years. He was a young, technology-savvy college student earning his undergrad degree in physics. He wanted to take a break from his studies and do something different, something adventurous while he was still young and single. When he returned to the United States and to all the comforts of home after two years of sleeping in a cot under the stars, sweating his ass off, and surrounded by mosquito netting, he was shocked at all the advances that took place in the short two years while he was gone, even simple things like the advances in iPhone technology. These are changes that we in the developed world have come to expect and take for granted to the point where we don't even notice them anymore.

In the last fifty years, mankind has seen developments in technology happen faster than we can keep track of, and now with the electronic and computer age in full swing, our desire to understand things which were once basic fundamentals of civilized life is no longer necessary. We don't have to learn how to do basic math because cash registers and calculators do it for us. We don't have to learn how to write in cursive because everything is printed from a keyboard, and when typing on the keyboard, we don't have to learn how to spell anymore because spell-checker does it for us (how many people actually attempt to sound out a word and spend thirty seconds or so trying to figure out their mistake before they use spell-checker? From my perspective and experience, very few). We don't need to know how to navigate by the stars, the sun, or even read a roadmap because GPS does it for us. We can't remember basic contact information because it's all stored in our cell phones. (Recently I had a fourteen-year-old student who was not picked up from class. When I told him to call his mom, he said he didn't have his cell phone with him and didn't know his mom's cell number, his home phone number, or his address. When I was eight years old, I knew my phone number and my address, and so did all the other kids.) We don't have interpersonal communication skills because everything is done over the Internet with our faces glued to our cell phones. Recently I saw two different TV ads illustrating the latest and greatest advancements in automobile technology. One feature was a sensor on the front bumper that would automatically brake if your car got too close to an object in front of it. Another innovation had sensors that beeped if your car drifted over the centerline. These improvements, like the invention of automatic high beam dimmers, all arose from a growing concern that people are obviously getting too distracted to drive. So now we have rumble strips and reflective bumps that warn us if we are going off the side of the road, beepers that tell us we're crossing the center line and sensors that will automatically brake for us. I've got a better idea: put away the lipstick and mirror and drive; stop fucking with the CD player, put two hands on the wheel, and drive; stop texting, check your blind spots, hang up, and drive! But no, we can't do that. After all, we have technology to do it for us.

One of many classic examples of this dependence on technology would be the advancements in aviation since the 1940s. After World War II, military aviation transformed from propeller-driven aircraft to jet engine technology, and over the next couple of decades, computer technology was implemented into military aircraft and weaponry. During the Korean War, fighter pilots relied on manually operated machine guns and cannons to engage the enemy. By the time the Vietnam War came around, military strategists and designers relied so heavily on air-to-air missiles for aerial combat that they didn't even put guns on the F-4 Phantom, the premier fighter in the Vietnam War. Pilots relied solely on air-to-air missiles, often shooting down their adversaries by locking

onto them from a radar screen without any visual contact whatsoever. As a result, the pilot kill ratio dropped significantly from
Korea to Vietnam, primarily because pilots were trained to rely
solely on their missile guidance systems and had lost much of their
dogfighting skills. The military brass finally recognized the unintended consequence of removing guns from fighter planes and
allowing pilots to rely solely on computer technology. This is one
of the primary reasons why the Top Gun school was started in
Miramar, California: to help pilots get back in touch with their
intuitive flying skills.

Many commercial airplane disasters from the last several decades have been a result of "pilot error." Pilots rely so heavily on
computers to fly the damn planes, when the shit hits the fan no
one in the cockpit knows how to deal with it. I am convinced that
if Captain Sully did not have superb stick-and-rudder skills from
years of flying gliders as a hobby, we would not be referring to the
downing of flight US Air 1549 as "The Miracle on the Hudson."

And if you don't believe that we are losing our most basic
intuitive survival instincts by allowing technology to take over,
then how is it that terrorists, with nothing more than box cutters,
were able to simultaneously hijack four commercial airliners and
take out the World Trade Center and part of the Pentagon, killing
nearly three thousand people? How is it that we allowed a piece
of foam insulation the size of a briefcase, weighing roughly two
pounds, to destroy the Space Shuttle Columbia? NASA personnel were aware of the foam strike shortly after launch, but when
it was brought to the attention of NASA upper management and
requested that, while in orbit, the wing of the Space Shuttle be in-
spected for potential damage, it was deemed unnecessary because
a small, lightweight piece of foam like that could never do any
significant damage to one of the most technologically advanced
pieces of machinery that man has ever created. In Vietnam, it was

B52s and the Airborne Cavalry versus the Ho Chi Minh trail. In the 1980s, it was the Afghans, with a little help from "Good Time" Charlie versus the Russian army. And again, I think we all know how those turned out.

We have allowed technology and the modern-day computer age to take over and consume our lives without the innate desire to understand it. For millions of years up until fifty to sixty years ago, when economic prosperity, the baby boomers, and the computer age came crashing down upon us, people survived on instinct, hard work, and common sense. My great-grandfather, who home-steaded in South Dakota in the 1870s, was a simple, uneducated, hardworking man of conviction. He had common sense and knew how to take care of his family while living off the land. Today no one feels the burning desire to learn how to live off the land because we have technology, all the comforts of home, and Big Brother to do it for us. As a result, we could not care less as long as we have our electricity to power the microwave and the home entertainment center.

Yes, ladies and gentlemen, we are losing our most basic, intuitive survival instincts that have been innate in our ancestors since the beginning of time. We have our increasingly adapting entitlement mentality so we don't have to aspire to anything—it will just be provided for us. Technology has created expectations in our daily lives that have transposed into demands, which have made us lazy, complacent, lethargic, and impatient as ever to the point where we don't care about anything as long as it works (Why is the Internet running so slowly, and who put the Pop-Tart in the DVD player?). The cause and effect, the unintended consequence of this wonderfully technological world we live in is that we, Homo sapiens, are getting dumber. We no longer have a strong work ethic, and if something doesn't come easily to us, we give up until someone fixes it for us—it's not my job! We have lost all our fundamental survival instincts because technology does it for us, and as soon as something breaks, we're lost until the technician comes to fix it.

Change isn't bad; change is inevitable. What we do with the change is the crime. How we take it for granted, how we abuse it, how we allow it to consume us without regard for the consequences—that is the crime!

When the next earthquake causes a massive tsunami that takes out everything from Jacksonville to Kennebunkport, or the next Midwest one hundred-year flood becomes a thousand-year flood, or the next meteor of any significant size strikes the earth, or the next catastrophic earthquake (you know, "the big one" that they have been predicting for some time now) rips California into the Pacific, or any of those other disasters that no one thinks will ever happen, or at least never happen to *them*, our only hope for survival will be that we have an Eagle Scout at our side, telling us what and what not to do.

Common sense, a basic, fundamental, and innate instinct in all life, is no longer "common" in the human species. It's now a virtue to be sought after and revered like the archeological discovery of a long lost civilization. It would not surprise me if twenty to thirty years from now a course on common sense is offered for college credit, just like customer service classes are offered today. Today we find ourselves at an evolutional turning point where Homo sapiens no longer have the ability, the intelligence, to deal with our most basic societal problems, and the moral dilemmas of tomorrow will be complicated tenfold by our own inability to deal with them now. At the same time, we humans are getting dumber by the decade. The societal exponential curve between human intelligence and societal problems is growing farther and farther apart. The day when the curve reverses its course, begins to merge back together, and the lines of human intelligence and the ability to solve societal problems once again intersect, is nowhere in sight. But that's OK because, as we all know, technology will save us!

Soylent Green is people!
—*Soylent Green*, the movie

History Repeats Itself

ince the dawn of man, history has repeated itself. Mother Nature has repeated herself, and mankind has repeated itself thousands of times over. Unfortunately when we are talking about mankind repeating itself, we're typically speaking about the mistakes we have made along the way, not our ability to learn from these mistakes. Learning from our mistakes is a fundamental concept of life that we try to instill in our children as they grow, and yet civilization as a whole doesn't seem to get it. So it's no surprise that children grow up to be just like us, creating a vicious cycle of destruction that will continue until we do ourselves in for good.

So if we humans have been repeating ourselves since the dawn of civilization, then what's the big deal if we're doing it again? The big deal is that we live in a much smaller and much more dangerous world; a world of nuclear proliferation where one country can wipe out the other side of the earth in a matter of hours. The big deal is that the problems we face today, most of which we have created ourselves, require intelligent and rational minds to address them. The big deal is that with all this going on, Homo sapiens are getting dumber, not smarter. As the worldly problems of today become significantly more serious, we humans become more stupid at an increasing rate. That's the big deal!

Take the Great American Depression of the '20s, '30s, and early '40s, for instance. Think that will never happen again? If so, you are either asleep at the wheel or simply in denial of what's going on in the world around you. The signs are everywhere, but as Spanish philosopher George Santayana once said, "Those who cannot remember the past are condemned to repeat it."[1] I believe we *do* remember the past; we're simply in denial of the fact that it can happen to us. We really don't care about the big picture or what's going on around us as long as we get our paychecks or our entitlements so we can buy things we can't afford, perpetuating our fiscally irresponsible month-to-month lifestyle, hastening the inevitable. Just as World War I became known as "The War to End All Wars" (and I think we all know how that turned out), the next Great Depression will become known as "The Great, Great Depression to End All Depressions." This monumental global collapse just waiting to happen is right around the corner and will be a hundred times worse than the last. I say that for several reasons. First, we now live in a global economy where one country's financial situation has a much greater impact on the rest of the world. With most of the developed world broke and printing money it doesn't have, when the crisis hits, it will be a global depression the likes of which has never been seen or even imagined. Secondly, we have been kicking the fiscal can down Wall Street for so long that the hole from which we will have to emerge is immense; we can't even see the gravedigger anymore, only the end of his shovel as he throws dirt onto the ground as fast as he can. And third, if people jumped out of windows when the stock market crashed in 1929, what do you think they will do now? An emotionally weak and spoiled society will be committing atrocities like you have never seen: rampant murder, suicide, murder and suicide, murder for hire, mercy killings (to spare people the pain of years of indiscretion), looting, and robbery that will last for decades. And, of course, the response will be for Big Brother government to seize more control of our lives, even though it will be Big Brother government that is primarily responsible for the depression to begin with. Or was it *us* who allowed government to get away with it? And if the last Great Depression lasted over ten years and took a huge expanse of government and a world war to get us out of it, what do you think it will take to pull us out of the next one? It's the roaring '20s all over again. So just live it up, people, because it could never happen to us!

Do you really think that when the residents of the Sendai Region of Japan woke up on March 11, 2011, they ever considered the possibility that by lunch their worlds would change forever as a result of a catastrophic tsunami? Do you think that any of the passengers on the Titanic, while sipping coffee in the dining room on the evening of April 14, 1912, thought for a second that in six hours most of them would be dead? Of course not! After all, they were unsinkable. Do you think any of the citizens of Pompeii woke up on the morning of August 24, AD 79, and figured that by dinner, they would be toast? Of course not. Have you taken a look at the Gulf of Naples today, and the area immediately surrounding Mount Vesuvius? Nobody worried about it in AD 79 and nobody's worrying about it in 2013 because it could never happen to them.

No one is sitting around worrying about all the warning signs of how today's society is looking more and more like life in Rome during the waning days of the empire. Instead, we're contributing to the decline by turning our heads and saying, "That's not my problem. I can't be bothered with it because I've got to get Sophia to dance class and Maverick to karate. And besides, it will always happen to someone else, not me!"

When in Rome, do as the Romans do!

WARNING
DISCLAIMER
The remainder of this book is not for the weak of heart.

If you are of sound body and mind, have common sense, are not brainwashed, look at the world objectively, and have the ability to think independently,

Then stop here, and *do not* read the remainder of this book.

Side effects may include: Nausea; Coughing; Vomiting; Diarrhea; Loss of Appetite; Sore Throat; Irritable Bowel Syndrome; Depression; Suicide; Memory Loss; Severe or Persistent Dizziness; Flushing; Headache; Heartburn; Rash; Hives; Itching; Difficulty Breathing; Tightness in the Chest; Swelling of the Mouth, Face, Lips or Tongue; Memory Loss; Dry Mouth; Chest Pain; Fainting; Fast or Irregular Heartbeat; Numbness of an Arm or Leg; Ringing in the Ears; Seizures; Blurriness in one or both eyes; Eye Floaters; Eye Twitching; Memory Loss; Trouble Sleeping; Delusions; Hallucinations; Frequent Urination; Red, Swollen, Peeling or Blistering Skin; Shortness of Breath; Muscle Spasms; Memory Loss; Nose or Throat Irritation; Sluggishness; Abnormal Thinking; Constipation; Decreased Sexual Desire or Ability; Absent Menstrual Period; Black, Tarry, or Bloody Stools; Memory Loss; Decreased Coordination; New or Worsening Agitation; Panic Attacks; Aggressiveness; Decreased Concentration; Impulsiveness; Painful Erections; Tremors; Memory Loss; Unusual Bruising or Bleeding; Moodiness; Yellowing of the Skin or Eyes; Dark Urine; Back Pain; Memory Loss; Sinus Inflammation; and Memory Loss.

THIS IS NOT A COMPLETE LIST OF ALL THE SIDE EFFECTS THAT MAY OCCUR

!!!! CONTINUE AT YOUR OWN RISK!!!!

Writers, editors, publishers assume *no* risk of responsibility for the actions of the reader or actions taken on behalf of the reader!

!!!! THE READER BEARS ALL RISKS OF RESPONSIBILITY!!!!

The Owl and the Pussycat

"Sweden to Adopt Bestiality Ban," June 2013
Sweden will next year introduce a total ban on bestiality, which until now has only been illegal if cruelty to the animal could be proven, the government said Thursday… Until now, bestiality was illegal in Sweden only if it could be proven that the animal had been subjected to suffering.[1]

That kind of gives a whole new meaning to the phrase "animal husbandry," doesn't it? What amazes me is that bestiality (or zoophilia, as it is also known), the act of having sex with animals, in and of itself, is not considered cruelty to animals. Many of the guidelines that determine whether or not sex with an animal is cruel revolve around the questions, "does it harm the animal?" or, "does the animal enjoy it?" (As if we know what an animal thinks or feels about being violated by a human.) I thought most animals had to be in *heat* in order to be willing participants in sex with their own kind, not to mention humans, but what do I know? Maybe if we could get bestiality aficionados to have sex with praying mantises, the problem would take care of itself.

Sweden's ban comes on the heels of a European Union directive to ban bestiality and follows suit behind Germany, Britain,

France, and Switzerland to do the same. I suppose putting this ban in place should be considered a step in the right direction, but if you stop to consider that bestiality has become so popular that major nations now have to address it by passing laws that forbid it, then it seems more patronizing than gratuitous. Besides, having laws in place will only mean that people will now have to be more discrete about their carnal behavior.

Another article in the *Huffington Post*, titled "Erotic Zoos Prompt Germany to Reinstate Bestiality Laws," pretty much says it all:

> The Daily Telegraph reports that bestiality laws have been off the books in Germany since 1969, but Agriculture Minister Ilse Aigner has agreed to support a law that would make it illegal for people to "use (animals) for their own sexual activities or sexual acts of third parties." The proposed law would also ban the "pimping" of animals to others. The Daily Mail ties this decision to address bestiality to the recent rise of erotic zoos, where "people can visit to abuse animals ranging from llamas to goats," the paper reports...The new law would ban these so-called "animal brothels" and also make it illegal to train animals for sex with humans.[2]

And, of course, the criminalization of bestiality has brought about a great debate as supporters of this animalistic behavior have come out of the barnyard to protect their fragile way of life. The Huffington article continues, "The proposed legislation has ruffled the feathers of zoophilia advocates such as Michael Kiok, who told the German newspaper *die Tageszeitung* that 'mere morals have no place in law.'" Apparently morals aren't a big issue with Mr. Kiok and a growing number of bestiality supporters, in or outside the law.

Another such debate on the website Debate.org (www.debate.org) posed such fanciful arguments as: "Having sex with animals would be no less cruel than eating them; It is no more dangerous than sleeping with a sex worker; It would cut down on prostitution and human trafficking; If it does give birth to a new industry, the government can tax the **** out of it; Legalizing bestiality would make it safer for those who already practice it."[3] Isn't that terrific? We already have "animal brothels" and the "pimping" of animals, so trading human prostitution for goat prostitution is the great moral and intellectual compromise we're making here? *Great!* I guess Woody Allen was right when he said, "I'd call him a sadistic, hippophilic necrophile, but that would be beating a dead horse."[4]

"Swiss Experts Say Plants Have Rights Too," April 2008

Plants need protection from maltreatment and pollution, government experts said on Monday. A report by the government-appointed Federal Ethics Committee on Non-Human Biotechnology (ECNH) described interfering with plants without a valid reason as "morally inadmissible." The committee looked at ethical views held on plants and issues of how their use could be justified. It said that from a wider perspective, "all action involving plants for the preservation of the human race was morally justified." A majority of the committee found that genetic modification of a plant did not contradict the idea of its "dignity" if it did not harm its adaptive or reproductive capacities, adding that the patented use of plants was acceptable. The ECNH was appointed to give an ethical perspective on the field of non-human biotechnology and gene technology and develop proposals on the principle of the dignity of creatures.[5]

OK, wait a minute. I want to make sure I'm getting this straight. The report says "interfering with plants without a valid reason as 'morally inadmissible.'" So a farmer is fine to harvest his fields, but if the farmer picks a blade of grass, puts it between his thumbs, holds it to his mouth, and whistles just for the hell of it, this is *morally inadmissible*? The report turns right around and says, "A majority of the committee found that genetic modification of a plant did not contradict the idea of its 'dignity' if it did not harm its adaptive or reproductive capacities, adding that the patented use of plants was acceptable." This is yet another perfect example of the absurdity of our intellectual state of mind, and how we disingenuously justify everything for our own means. We can't indiscriminately destroy plants or weeds, but it's perfectly fine to *genetically modify* them, as if we know how the plant feels and what's best for it. (How about we men tell our women that they need to be genetically modified by having Botox lip injections to make them prettier, and they just need to do it because we know what's best for them?)

And plants now have *dignity*? Next humans will determine that plants have a soul, and we will be debating which religion best reflects their *nature* and which religion they *identify* with. Since Switzerland now has to kill all vegetables in a *dignified* and *respectful* way, I assume all the plants are kosher and practice Judaism. Put a yarmulke on that head of cabbage, will ya?

The most troubling thought concerning this report is that the government of an industrialized, leading nation in this world of ours is spending time, money, and resources debating whether or not they should give plants the same rights as humans. It's no wonder we can't eradicate world hunger or the spread of AIDS—we are too busy debating whether or not your five-year-old daughter has the right to pick a dandelion and blow its seeds into the air just because it's fun, and it's what kids do. Will parents now be held accountable in a court of law for their child's criminal dandelion behavior?

A blog entry that followed the article, written by M. Dorothy of Switzerland, said, "Perhaps the Swiss government should focus on giving women equal rights before plants." I assume Dorothy was referring to the fact that Switzerland did not give women the right to vote until 1971. A bit behind the curve on human rights, wouldn't you say? Well done, Dorothy, well done!

Is it just me or does anyone else see the absurdity and the hypocrisy in all of this? How long will it be before we start hearing things like "I didn't have sexual relations with that goat!" or "Your honor, I stepped on the grass by accident, I swear!"

These stories are very real, very sad, and very scary examples of how and why we, as a species, have lost our minds and justify everything for our own benefit. It's not really about the plants or the animals; it's all about making us humans feel good about ourselves. We want to feel like we're accomplishing something and changing the world for the better when all we're doing is patting ourselves on the back and telling ourselves what a great job we're doing, all the while children are starving in third world countries. Our modern-day reality is becoming nothing more than a nonsensical poem that is hastily slipping into a nonsensical nightmare from which we may never awaken.

> *They dined on mince, and slices of quince,*
> *Which they ate with a runcible spoon;*
> *And hand in hand, on the edge of the sand,*
> *They danced by the light of the moon,*
> *The moon,*
> *The moon,*
> *They danced by the light of the moon.*
> —"The Owl and the Pussycat" by Edward Lear

What's So Confusing About Gender Confusion?

*H*ere's one of those topics that's going to get me in trouble, but after delving into all the other societal misfits (to put it politely) while writing this book, I really don't care. So let me explain something: if you have a penis, you're a dude, and if you have a vagina, you're a dudette. Yes, ladies and gentlemen, it really is that simple. This is one of those areas where we humans have muddied the waters so much that we can't see the tits for the pectoral.

It's true that some people have hormonal imbalances of estrogen or testosterone, or certain psychological conditions, or perhaps even a variant in their DNA that makes them behave like the opposite sex, or *feel* like the opposite sex, or even *believe* that they are the opposite sex, and so they become confused about their sexuality. So go off and experiment with your sexuality. Try homosexuality or lesbianism, if that's the case. Now if you're an honest-to-goodness hermaphrodite, then you've got something to brag about! But show me a real Homo sapien hermaphrodite, and I'll show you a snail who hates to have a good time with itself, if you know what I mean.

I would like to begin with a recent story in the *Huffington Post* titled "Germany to Offer Third Gender Option on Birth Certificates." The article starts by saying:

As of November [2013], Germany will be the first country in Europe to offer a "third gender" distinction on its birth certificates. A new German law stipulates that children who are born of indeterminate gender no longer have to be categorized as "male" or "female." Instead, parents can choose to leave the space blank on their child's birth certificate...Those individuals can eventually decide whether to identify as male, female or neither.[1]

Great! I thought that deciphering between a penis and a vagina was Doctor 101, but apparently educated doctors, politicians, and the rest of humanity doesn't seem to understand the difference between anatomical sexuality and hormonal sexuality.

Another story published October 17, 2011 on Foxnews.com, titled "Controversial Therapy for Pre-Teen Transgender Patient Raises Questions," leaps right into the anatomical vs hormonal sexuality debate. The article begins:

A lesbian couple in California who say their 11-year-old son Tommy who wants to be a girl named Tammy are giving their child hormone blockers that delay the onset of puberty—so that he can have more time to decide if he wants to change his gender. The couple's supporters say the Hormone Blocking Therapy has only minor side effects and is appropriate for a child who is unsure of his gender. "This is definitely a changing landscape for transgender youth," said Joel Baum, director of education and training for Gender Spectrum, a California-based non-profit group. "This is about giving kids and their families the opportunity to make the right decision."[2]

It may be possible that Tommy was born with a hormonal imbalance or DNA variant in his body that would cause him to behave this way, but is it also possible that Tommy's lesbian parents might have a smidgen of influence on Tommy's behavior? According to the American Academy of Pediatrics in an article published in HealthyChildren.org: "These gender role behaviors, including the toys children play with and activities in which they engage are influenced by how youngsters are raised and what expectations are made of them."[3] Gee, ya think?

I suppose what bothers me the most about this story (aside from the fact that it's a real story happening to a real kid in our lovely modern-day society, as opposed to some sick, twisted, and demented Stephen King novel or Quentin Tarantino movie) is that the parents are giving their eleven-year-old hormone blockers in order to "delay the onset of puberty—so that he can have more time to decide if he wants to change his gender." My question is, how can individuals even come to an informed conclusion about wanting to change their gender without going through puberty first? Without experiencing sexuality? Without experiencing relationships and dating and love and heartbreak? Without experiencing what it is that he (his parents) thinks he wants to change? Not to mention the fact that he's fucking eleven years old! Who among us knew anything about anything when we were eleven, particularly our sexuality? And keep in mind, we're not talking about his hormonal sexuality (whether he will grow up to be heterosexual or homosexual), we're talking about giving an eleven-year-old the right to change his anatomical sexuality! Someone please explain why this is not illegal? Why this is not criminal? But, of course, it's not illegal or criminal because *we* make it so. Does that mean if an eleven-year-old girl who has grown up with four brothers and shows a strong attraction to sports, wears jeans instead of dresses, and hangs around with the boys more than her girlfriends, and is a quintessential tomboy, that she should be given hormone blockers to see if, by chance, she would rather have a penis?

Tommy obviously has a penis and, therefore, is anatomically male. Whether or not he is hormonally showing feminine signs without the influence of his lesbian parents remains to be seen. Regardless of his parents' influence, why can't we let the kid be a kid, behave as he will, and after puberty, after he has seen and done a thing or two in his life, then he can decide if he wants to be heterosexual, homosexual, or transsexual. Why are we forcing the issue by giving him prescription drugs and hormone-blocking therapy at age eleven? After all, we have to be sixteen years old in order to be responsible enough to drive an automobile in the United States; we have to be eighteen to vote; at eighteen we are also legally adults, and can cut the apron strings, and make our own decisions; depending on the state you live in, you have to be at least sixteen to have consensual sex; at twenty-one years old, we can legally consume alcohol; and at eleven years old, apparently, we are mature enough to make decisions concerning our gender that will dramatically alter and change our world for the rest of our lives.

This attitude of giving children the option to responsibly choose which gender they associate with is going mainstream. It is yet another one of the one hundred pieces of the societal puzzle that is being removed, forever obscuring the picture of what we, as a civilization, are becoming.

Another one of many recent stories in the *Huffington Post* talks about a six-year-old Colorado first grader who was discriminated against because he couldn't use the girls' bathroom.[4] School officials were allowing the child to use gender neutral bathrooms, such as the one in the nurse's office or the teacher's lounge, but "Coy's parents feared she would be stigmatized and bullied." So they brought the issue before the Colorado Civil Rights Division, who ruled in favor of the parents. Coy, who has a penis, is now allowed to use the girl's bathroom, and of course that's great news because now we don't have to worry about him/her being "stigmatized and bullied." The article went on to say, "Coy was born a triplet with two sisters and identified as a girl before she began attending elementary school...At 5 months, she took a pink blanket meant for her sister Lily. Later, she showed little interest in toy cars and boy clothes with pictures of sports, monsters and dinosaurs on them." Well, of course, there's a good chance he's not going to identify with those things at that age because as the American Academy of Pediatrics says, "These gender role behaviors, including the toys children play with and activities in which they engage, are influenced by how youngsters are raised and what expectations are made of them." Do you really think being surrounded by mommy and his two twin sisters all day every day isn't going to have *any* influence on his behavior? If everyone around you is playing with dolls all day long, there's a good chance that you're going to pick up a doll and play with it too. But Coy's intelligent, progressive parents were convinced that by the time Coy was three or four years old (or whatever age Coy's parents became certain that they *knew* what Coy wanted to be) that he was unhappy with his gender, and it was Coy's *right* to begin fighting for something that he is completely incapable of understanding or truly knowing the consequences of the decisions that he (his parents) is making. An elderly person, who significantly changes his or her last will & testament in the waning days of his or her life will come under intense scrutiny, and once they are gone, there will be legal battles that often go on for years as to whether the person was of sound body and mind when the will was changed. Perhaps they were unfairly taken advantage of and under the influence or duress of a third party. But a six-year-old is perfectly capable of making those decisions on his own and is not influenced by others whatsoever. I find it astonishing that the parents would state in the article, "At 5 months, she took a pink blanket meant for her sister Lily." Seriously? This is one of the early defining moments that they are basing their decisions on? Coy must have been a highly evolved five-month-old genius to be able to consciously understand the whole "blue for boys and pink for girls" concept, and then turn around and deliberately choose the pink blanket over the blue one. Is it humanly possible that perhaps Coy's feeble, still undeveloped brain was just attracted to the brighter, more vibrant pink? Did anyone think of that as a possibility? What does a six-year-old know about sexuality anyway? They know that daddy has a wee-wee, mommy has a vajayjay, and that's about it. So someone please tell me why this behavior by the parents, by society, is not illegal? Why this is not criminal? As parents, we won't let our kids have dessert before they eat their peas, but it's OK for six-year-olds to decide which sex they identify with and which public bathroom is the most appropriate for them to use. Society should be put on lockdown until we can get our heads screwed on straight!

The good news is it won't be long before municipalities and local school districts will be absolved from the responsibility of all these indeterminate gender, gender neutral, transgender, and gender confusion issues of our children and will be able to get back to the daunting task of educating our kids. Leave it to California to lead the way into the abyss by passing "A.B. 1266, a K–12 transgender bill that will change the education code to specify that regardless of the gender listed on a piece of paper in the front office, a student can participate in sex-segregated activities, athletic teams, and yes, use bathroom facilities consistent with his or her gender identity."[5]

Has anyone stopped and thought about what the unintended consequences of this law might be? Does anyone have a clue what we're getting ourselves into? Does anyone care? We can't deal with normal everyday male/female, boyfriend/girlfriend, husband/wife relationships, and this just throws napalm on the fire.

If we, as a society, are allowing this gender confusion ideology to be indoctrinated into children as young as six and segue into our high schools, then it should come as no surprise that more and more esteemed institutions of higher education are providing students with gender neutral housing for students who don't know who or what they are. Many of these universities are upping the ante and are now offering to pay for students who wish to have sex changes (excuse me, gender reassignment surgeries) by offering it on their student health plans.[6] Since when did it become policy for universities to pay for students to have a sex change? What does this even remotely have to do with providing them with an education or basic health care? What memo did I miss? Maybe, just maybe, if we stop confusing the hell out of children when they are six years old, then maybe, just maybe, by the time they are adults they wouldn't be so confused about who or what they are.

I will leave you with an article that appeared on March 27, 2012 on www.usatodayeducate.com. While discussing the pro and con argument to gender neutral housing on college campuses, a junior at the University of Pennsylvania stated, "I think it's really positive in terms of thinking about gender critically in the United States. We aren't dividing ourselves along arbitrary lines anymore."[7]

Great! Millions of years of evolution and suddenly the existence of male and female is an "arbitrary" concept. *Great!*

Where Does It All End?

*L*ife in 1800 changed very little from 1750. Life in 1850 changed a smidgen from 1800. Life in 1900 changed quite a bit from 1850. Life in 1950 changed substantially from that of 1900. And life in 2000 was a paradigm shift from that of 1950. And if in 1950 no one imagined that in 2000 we would be walking around with a thing called a smartphone in our pockets that could answer every question we possibly had and could tell us our exact location on this planet at any given moment at the push of a button, then 2050 will bring advances so great, it will make 2000 look like the Stone Age.

Technology has advanced so rapidly in the last forty years that the average Homo sapien cannot intellectually keep up, yet that does not stop us from marching forward into the abyss. Many will argue that socially, the beginning of the end is already here. Economically we are teetering on the edge of a fiscal cliff, the likes of which mankind has never seen before. Morally...forget it. Culturally it's anyone's guess, if there is such a thing as culture anymore. And still, we keep marching on!

It wasn't too long ago that abortion was illegal. Then it was legal. But that wasn't good enough, so we pushed the envelope a little farther and it was OK to have late-term abortions, then partial-birth abortions, and then feticide. There have been stories about parents aborting fetuses simply because they don't have blue eyes or blond hair like the parents wanted. You think it stops there? Please! How long will it be before we are destroying fetuses for research? If we have the right to abort them anyway, it seems like an awful waste of human tissue. Let's put it to good use. Waste not, want not!

Human cloning is illegal, but I can assure you that it won't be for much longer. I give it another twenty years or so, and we will be getting accustomed to the idea of animal cloning. Twenty more years and human cloning will be perfectly fine. Twenty years after that, and it will not only be acceptable, but the practice of human cloning will be commonplace. Then what's the next evolution of that concept? Ever see the movie *The Island* with Ewan McGregor and Scarlett Johansson? We will be cloning ourselves just so we can harvest our own organs and tissues whenever we need it. Need a heart transplant? Well, by God, why not take it from a genetic reproduction of yourself without the hassles of finding a compatible donor? Think that's far-fetched? Think that will never happen? That the cloning issue suddenly stops at cloning? Please! If you look at historical trends, nothing ever reverses course and reverts back to how it used to be. It always moves forward. That's progress! After all, clones aren't real. "They're artificial reproductions of ourselves." That will be the legal justification of the future. Artificial reproductions genetically designed and created by us to serve our means, not theirs. This will be the slave trade of the twenty-second century!

What about the onslaught of transgender issues that are currently challenging the status quo? Give it a few decades and transgender will be old-school, and becoming a hermaphrodite will be the latest craze. Think about it, why wouldn't a self-absorbed society want the best of both worlds? Then you won't have to worry about which gender you associate with, you can simply pick the flavor of the week, or the moment!

What's the next evolution of bestiality? Let's ask our great, great, great-grandchildren one hundred years from now (assuming Homo sapiens are still around), and they will tell you it's their *right* to be married to a Satyr if they want to. It's their right to have centaur children if they wish. Where does it end? It never does! We continue to push the envelope simply because we can and simply because it's our right.

As a society, we don't *need* anything else, but we keep *wanting* more. If we have two hundred cable channels, we want five hundred. If we have a fifty-two-inch flat screen TV, we want an eighty-four-inch. If we make 50K a year, we want 70K. If we own a Toyota Corolla, we want an Avalon. If we have a good and loving wife, we want a mistress. If we have a 200K house, we want a 300K house. Nothing is ever good enough, so we keep pushing and pushing the envelope until the envelope can't be delivered anymore. Having dreams and desires is one thing, but when pursuing those dreams only makes us impatient, depressed, unappreciative, and hungry for more, then you have to stop and ask yourself, "What's the point?"

There is an old Buddhist proverb, mentioned earlier, that says, "There is no way to happiness. Happiness is the way." I know many wealthy people that are depressed and miserable. They keep chasing that artificial dream. They keep living that artificial lifestyle steeped in pop culture that they think is going to make them happy and it doesn't. All the while, their society around them crumbles.

I respect the Amish for knowing when to say "enough is enough," for looking at the world objectively and saying, "No, that's not where we want to go. That's not the society and culture we want our kids to be raised in. We're fine right where we are." It takes balls to turn away from the modern conveniences of today and say, "That's not what makes us happy, and mankind is proving that point every day."

I don't think I could be Amish. That lifestyle goes back a little too far for me. But I certainly appreciate it with great admiration. I could definitely go and live like that for a few weeks every year. It would be my therapy, my pilgrimage to get back to my roots, to keep it all in perspective: the money, the social status, the pop culture, and the lifestyle. That retreat would keep me in check, reminding me of what's important in life, what's worth discarding, and how to establish a true and everlasting appreciation for the things I do have. As for me, my modern-day Amish-ism began when I threw my TV out the window. That was the point where I said "enough is enough." I have tried to be intellectually honest with myself and continue to make changes (or "advancements to the past," as I like to call them) as I move forward with *my* life. To me, that's progress!

> "Life is really simple, but we insist on making it complicated."[1]
> —Confucius

Ad Nauseam: The End

I have to end this book now. I have to end it now because every day that goes by, I hear or see something that lends a sense of urgency to finishing this book. So much indigent and depraved information pours in every week, sometimes on a daily basis, that I can no longer keep up with it. Some of the information written here is already obsolete, even though it only happened a year or two before publishing.

And so, in closing, many of you may be asking, "So what's the big deal?" This has been going on since the beginning of civilization: society debating the social, economic, and moral decline going on among them; the older generation always blaming the younger generation for making a travesty of societal mores; and the younger generation blaming the old codgers for being "old-fashioned," "set in their ways," "a pain in the ass," and "out of touch with reality."

So what *is* the big deal? Why are we yacking on and on about something that has been yacked about since the beginning of civilization? We're yacking about it because in the 1960s, Elvis Presley's hips were banned from television for being too suggestive with too many hormonal teenage girls crooning and screaming over this man's overly provocative gyrations. Today, fifty years later, anyone, including unsupervised kids, can get all the porn they want at the push of a button on a smartphone that they carry in their pockets everywhere they go. That's the problem! And unfortunately, by the time we wake up from this nightmare, if we wake up at all, it will be too late. It will be over.

The societal exponential curve has reached terminal velocity in terms of Homo sapiens rationally, morally, and intellectually, dealing with our most basic and fundamental issues of the day. Modern-day technology has advanced so rapidly in the last four decades that we are no longer able to deal with it on a moral, or even an intellectual, level. Common sense is now a thing of the past. We rationalize and justify everything we do with the most disingenuous of reasons. We lie to ourselves to get what we want and to make our lives more comfortable simply because it's our right, without any regard for the consequences.

Einstein once said, "I fear the day that technology will surpass our human interaction. The world will have a generation of idiots."[1] I believe if Einstein were alive today, even he would be shocked at how fast it has happened.

If you lived anytime from the dawn of man up until the middle of the eighteenth century, just prior to the Industrial Revolution, you would have had to look back hundreds and hundreds of years to get a sense of significant progress and advances in technology, and there was certainly little or no progress in one's lifetime. Even if you were fortunate enough to live a long and prosperous life, you pretty much died in the same society you were born into. Oh, sure, you might have seen a sizeable piece of a colosseum, or an aqueduct, or a cathedral, or a pyramid, or a great wall, or some other monumental, man-made achievement being built before your very eyes over the course of your lifetime, but the technology that built those monuments to mankind were pretty much the same. People still used masons and hand tools to cut the stones. People still used horses as their primary mode of transportation. They still used sails to go where horses could not.

It wasn't until the Industrial Revolution, beginning in the late 1700s, that we saw the invention of the steam engine, which, after thousands and thousands of years, replaced horses with steam-powered locomotives and replaced sails with mechanically powered paddlewheels. Over the next hundred years, mankind began to see advances that most never dreamed of.

Da Vinci dreamed of a lot of things. He dreamed of flying, as did millions of people for thousands of years. Then one day in 1903, the Wright brothers made history with the first manned, powered flight, lasting a humbling twelve seconds over the sands of Kill Devil Hills, North Carolina. A very short sixty-five years later, mankind landed men on the moon and returned them to earth safely. That's a paradigm shift that is hard to beat.

In the past forty to fifty years, the societal exponential curve between technology and humanity has come apart like the cables of a suspension bridge (technology) separating from the roadway (humanity) at an ever-increasing rate. The cables (technology) have now reached the pinnacle of the supporting tower, in terms of humanity appropriately dealing with the advances in this field, and it is now beginning to implode as the cables begin their rapid descent downward, until technology comes crashing down on humanity like the Tacoma Narrows Bridge.

So what can be done about this situation? What can the masses do to reverse course? In my opinion, nothing! A very sad and simple reality is that history repeats itself. It *has* repeated itself since the beginning of civilization, and even though we know this to be true, quite frankly, we don't care, or at least don't care to say, "Enough is enough!" After all, we are too comfortable with our contemporary lifestyle, and we simply can't get enough of it.

Anne Frank was only fourteen years old when, on May 3, 1944, she wrote in her diary:

There is a destructive urge in people, the urge to rage, murder and kill. And until all of humanity, without exception, undergoes a metamorphosis, wars will continue to be waged, and everything that has been carefully built up, cultivated and grown will be cut down and destroyed, only to start all over again![2]

Quite intuitive for a fourteen-year-old young woman. Apparently she, too, knew something that we can't seem to grasp. Personally, I am humbled and ashamed to be taught such a remedial and elementary lesson of life by someone so young and innocent.

Perhaps that's where the hope, if there is any, lies: in the innocence of youth. Children aren't inherently racist. They just want to play with other kids; they don't care what color they are. Children don't care who's ugly and who's not, because they don't know what that is. They don't care if their mama is 350 pounds, because they love her unconditionally. (I would like to think that the opposite is always true, but sometimes you have to wonder.) It is their teachers, and I don't mean teachers in the "formal education" sense of the word, I mean all of us, who fill their heads with these misgivings.

So, if the teachers, the adults, are the corrupt ones, what can we do? The great conundrum is that there are, of course, many things we can do, but we won't. Like the Roman Empire after hundreds of years of being top dog, we have become complacent. We got lazy and are getting lazier by the day, we're dropping our guard, we're getting too comfortable, and, quite frankly, we don't care.

I am afraid that the time when "everything that has been carefully built up, cultivated and grown will be cut down and destroyed, only to start all over again" is quickly approaching. It *has* been approaching for decades now. The deterioration of Homo sapiens is an inherent and self-fulfilling prophecy of the human race.

It's a deterioration that, like aging, occurs so gradually right before our eyes that we are in denial, or we dismiss it as "not that bad." Then one day we wake up, look in the mirror, and wonder, "What the hell happened?" By then it's too late to do anything about it, or at least that's our justification of it, and we simply accept it as "the norm." Some will argue that it's just change, and change is inevitable. This is true: change *is* inevitable. But it's what we, Homo sapiens, do with the change that is the problem.

I presume that most people who read this book will be pissed off about it, or get a kick out of it, or perhaps a little of both. But few will actually be empathetic, put the shoe on the other foot, or look in the mirror to see how *they* are contributing to the decline of their genealogy and to the whole of the human race. No, it's always the other guy's fault. The fact that we hang around with the other guy is inconsequential. The fact that we are a willing participant in the lifestyle and pop culture that we have created with the other guy is inconsequential. Well, I am here to tell you, ladies and gentlemen, that, in my humble opinion, we *are* the problem. Until we, as individuals, look in the mirror and accept a little (actually a lot) responsibility and constructive criticism, then we are destined to repeat history on a monumental scale the human race has never experienced before.

So, at significant risk of changing the world for the better, I will be the first to admit my faults. I will be the first to walk the plank for the sake of all Homo sapiens and for the sake of setting a standard of conduct for myself in the hopes of inspiring the masses to reverse course and do the same.

The Homo Sapien Creed

1. **Treat others as you would like to be treated**: Go out of your way to be caring and compassionate to people,

and not just every once in a while so that you feel good about yourself. It's not about you. It's about what you leave behind.

2. **Stick by your principles**: Do this without fail. This one might be a little fuzzy for some folks since one man's principles are another man's trash. So if you're a little confused about what good strong morals and principles are, go ask a six-year-old about right from wrong, and they can help you figure it out.

3. **Throw your TV out the window**: Start reading and writing, learn a foreign language, go back to school; volunteer your time to a worthy cause. Do something, anything, other than rotting your brain and wilting away in front of the TV.

4. **Take responsibility for your actions**: Do this always!

5. **Rugged Individualism**: Don't point a finger or blame any individual or entity for your failures. Sometimes we get lucky, and sometimes we get shit on. That's life! Stop blaming others, learn from your mistakes, and get back in the saddle.

6. **Vote**: Get involved or stop complaining! Don't just educate yourself on the talking points. Make sure you understand both sides of every issue, and you understand the consequences and unintended consequences of your decisions.

7. **Live in a fiscally responsible manner:** Don't live beyond your financial means. Plan and take responsibility for your financial future and retirement. Don't bank on the government to do it for you.

8. **Humility**: This goes a long way.
9. **Look in the mirror**: Be empathetic and look at your own actions before criticizing others.
10. **Practice these *daily***: Live them! Pass them on!

The Solution Begins With <u>You</u>.

Happy Hunting!

The End

is near!

Notes

Introduction
[1] Mark Twain. "Mark Twain Quotes." Goodreads.com. Accessed April 17, 2014. http://www.goodreads.com/quotes/78468.

Section 1: The Birthing Canal
In The Beginning...There Was Reason
[1] John F. Kennedy. "Historic Speeches." John F. Kennedy Presidential Library and Museum (January 20, 1961). Accessed April 17, 2014. http://jfklibrary.org/.

The Color Purple
[1] *George Carlin It's Bad For Ya*. Directed byRocco Urbisci (2008, HBO Motion Picture).

Supersize Me!
[1] Heart.org. "What is Childhood Obesity?" Heart.org. Accessed April 18, 2014. http://www.heart.org/HEARTORG/GettingHealthy/HealthierKids/ChildhoodObesity/What-is-childhood-obesity_UCM_304347_Article.jps.
[2] Trevor Stokes. "Bloomberg Defends Soda Ban Plan: We're Not Taking Away Your Freedoms." Today.com (June 1, 2012). Accessed April 18, 2014. http://www.today.com/health/bloomberg-defends-soda-ban-plan-were-not-taking-away-your-807138.

Imagine That!

[1] Po Bronson and Ashley Merryman. "The Creativity Crisis." TheDailyBeast. com (July 10, 2010). Accessed June 30, 2012. http://www.thedailybeast.com/ newsweek/2010/07/10/the-creativity-crisis.html.

[2] Britannica. "The Decline if Creativity in the United States: 5 Questions for Educational Psychologist." Britannica.com (October 18, 2010). Accessed June 30, 2012. http://www.britannica.com/blogs/2010/10/the-decline-of-creativity-in-the-united-states-5-questions-for-educational-psychologist-kyung-hee-kim/.

A Spoonful of Sugar Helps the Medicine Go Down

[1] Centers for Disease Control and Prevention. "Why are Autism Spectrum Disorders Increasing?" CDC.gov (Last reviewed April 16, 2012). Accessed April 18, 2014. http://www.cdc.gov/features/autismprevalence/.

[2] Centers for Disease Control and Prevention. "Childhood Obesity Facts." CDC.gov (Last reviewed February 27, 2014). Accessed April 18, 2014. http://www.cdc.gov/healthyyouth/obesity/facts.htm.

[3] Centers for Disease Control and Prevention. "Children and Diabetes-More Information." CDC.gov (Last reviewed September 25, 2013). Accessed April 18, 2014. http://www.cdc.gov/diabetes/projects/cda2.htm.

[4] Lara J. Akinbami. "The State of Childhood Asthma, United States, 1980-2005." Advance Data From Vital and Health Statistics, no. 381 (2006). CDC. gov. Accessed April 18, 2014. http://www.cdc.gov/nchs/data/ad/ad381.pdf.

[5] Centers for Disease Control and Prevention. "ADHD: Resources are Available." CDC.gov (Last reviewed August 23, 2012. Accessed April 18, 2014. http://www.cdc.gov/features/adhdresources/.

[6] Centers for Disease Control and Prevention. "National Center on Birth Defects and Developmental Disabilities." CDC.gov (Last reviewed August 14, 2012). Accessed February 28, 2013. http://www.cdc.gov/ncbddd/features/birthdefects-dd-keyfindings.html.

[7] Environmental Protection Agency. "What You Need to Know about Mercury in Fish and Shellfish." EPA.gov (Last updated November 20, 2013). Accessed

April 19, 2014. http://water.epa.gov/scitech/swguidance/fishshellfish/outreach/advice_index.cfm.

[8] David DiSalvo. "What Eating Too Much Sugar Does To Your Brain." Forbes.com (April 1, 2012). Accessed November 11, 2012. http://www.forbes.com/sites/daviddisalvo/2012/04/01/what-eating-too-much-sugar-does-to-your-brain/.

[9] Drugs.com. "Ritalin." Drugs.com (Last revised July 7, 2010). Accessed March 16, 2013. http://www.drugs.com/ritalin.html.

Whatcha Gonna Do When They Come for You?

[1] New York Times. "Lindbergh Baby Kidnapped from Home of Parents on Farm Near Princeton; Taken from his Crib; Wide Search On." *On This Day*. NYTimes.com. Accessed April 19, 2014. http://www.nytimes.com/learning/general/onthisday/big/0301.html.

[2] Wikipedia. "Lindbergh Kidnapping." Wikipedia.org (Last modified April 19, 2014). Accessed April 21, 2014. http://en.wikipedia.org/wiki/Lindbergh_kidnapping.

[3] Wikipedia. "AMBER Alert." Wikipedia.org (Last modified October 18, 2012). Accessed November 11, 2012. http://en.wikipedia.org/wiki/AMBER_Alert.

Section 2: The Rise of the Machines
Your Pubes Are Showing

[1] Sigmund Freud. "Sigmund Freud Children Parents Quotes." SearchQuotes.com. Accessed April 21, 2014. http://www.searchquotes.com/search/Sigmund_Freud_Children_Parents/.

Are You Smarter Than a Fifth Grader?

[1] VideoBash.com. "Are You Smarter than a 5th Grader 352 Feet in a Yard." *YouTube* video, 4:45, July 21, 2011. https://www.youtube.com/watch?v=xHgkbdXnMiY.

[2] Macrina Cooper-White. "People Getting Dumber? Human Intelligence Has Declined Since Victorian Era, Research Suggests." HuffingtonPost.com (May

22, 2013). Accessed August 13, 2013. http://huffingtonpost.com/2013/05/22/people-getting-dumber-human-intelligence-victoria-era_n_3293846.html.

[3] Christina Huffington. "Single Motherhood Increases Dramatically For Certain Demographics, Census Bureau Reports." HuffingtonPost.com (Updated May 2, 2013). Accessed August 30, 2013. http://www.huffingtonpost.com/2013/05/01/single-motherhood-increases-census-report_n_3195455.html.

[4] Statistic Brain. "High School Dropout Statistics." StatisticBrain.com (Research date April 28, 2013). Accessed August 15, 2013. http://www.statisticbrain.com/high-school-dropout-statistics/.

[5] Wikipedia. "Idiocracy." Wikipedia.org (Last modified April 18, 2014). Accessed April 21, 2014. http://en.wikipedia.org/wiki/Idiocracy.

Please Pass the Roll Model—Pleeeese!

[1] ChildStats.gov. "America's Children: Key National Indicators of Well-Being, 2013 – Family Structure and Children's Living Arrangements." ChildStats.gov. (2013). Accessed August 29, 2013. http://www.childstats.gov/americaschildren/famsoc1.asp.

[2] The Fatherless Generation. "The Fatherless Generation-Statistics." TheFatherlessGenerationwordpress.com. Accessed August 29, 2013. http://thefatherlessgeneration.wordpress.com/statistics/.

[3] Goodreads. "Quotes About Role Models." Goodreads.com. Accessed August 28, 2013. http://www.goodreads.com/quotes/tag/role-models.

The Scarlet Letter

[1] Centers for Disease Control and Prevention. "About Teen Pregnancy." CDC.gov (Last updated November 21, 2012). Accessed August 30, 2013. http://cdc.gov/teenpregnancy/aboutteenpreg.htm.

[2] Centers for Disease Control and Prevention. "Sexual Risk Behavior: HIV, STD, & Teen Pregnancy Prevention." CDC.gov (Last updated August 26, 2013). Accessed August 31, 2013. http://www.cdc.gov/HealthyYouth/sexualbehaviors/.

³ Centers for Disease Control and Prevention. "STD Trends in the United States, 2011 National Data for Chlamydia, Gonorrhea, and Syphilis." CDC. gov. (March 2013). Accessed April 21, 2014. http://www.cdc.gov/std/stats11/trends-2011.pdf.

⁴ Nicole Solofsky. "14 Teen Pregnancies That Happened On Scripted TV Shows." OKMagazine.com (April 25, 2013). Accessed September 4, 2013. http://ok-magazine.com/photos/14-teen-pregnancies-happened-scripted-tv-shows/photo/1000601013/.

⁵ ENigerianNews. "I Am Pregnant with My Dad's Baby and We are Madly In love with Each Other." ENigerianNews.blogspot.com (April 30, 2012). Accessed April 21, 2014. http://enigerianews.blogspot.com/2012/04/i-am-pregnant-with-my-dads-baby-and-we.html.

We Are All Adam Lanza's Mother

¹ Wikipedia. "Bath School Disaster." Wikipedia.org (Last modified April 20, 2014). Accessed April 21, 2014. http://en.wikipedia.org/wiki/Bath_School_disaster.

² Wikipedia. "Charles Whitman." Wikipedia.org (Last modified April 21, 2014). Accessed April 21, 2014. http://en.wikipedia.org/wiki/Charles_Whitman.

³ Wikipedia. "List of school shootings in the United States." Wikipedia.org (Last modified September 6, 2013). Accessed September 7, 2013. http://en.wikipedia.org/wiki/List_of_school_shootings_in_the_United_States.

Section 3: Planet of the Apes

Take This Job and Love It

¹ National Day Calendar. "What National Day is Today?" National Day Calendar.com Accessed August 22, 2013. http://nationaldaycalendar.com/.

² Martin Luther King, Jr. "What Is Your Life's Blueprint?" Seattle Times.com Accessed April 21, 2014. http://seattletimes.com/special/mlk/king/words/blueprint.html.

Sign, Sign, Everywhere's a Sign

[1] National Coffee Association. "How To Brew Coffee." NACAUSA.org. Accessed April 22, 2014. http://www.ncausa.org/i4a/pages/index.cfm?pageid=71.

[2] RinkWorks. "Things People Said: Warning Labels." RinksWorks.com. Accessed November 19, 2012. http://www.rinkworks.com/said/warnings.shtml.

Super Morbidly Obese

[1] Centers for Disease Control and Prevention. "2009 H1N1 Flu In The News." CDC.gov (Last reviewed March 16, 2010). Accessed April 22, 2014. http://www.cdc.gov/h1n1flu/in_the_news/obesity_qa.htm.

Doctor, Doctor, Give Me the News!

[1] Sigmund Freud. "Sigmund Freud Children Parents Quotes." SearchQuotes.com. Accessed April 21, 2014. http://www.searchquotes.com/search/Sigmund_Freud_Children_Parents/.

[2] Centers for Disease Control and Prevention. "Children's Mental Health - New Report." (Last updated May 21, 2013). Accessed September 22, 2013. http://www.cdc.gov/features/childrensmentalhealth/.

[3] Mayo Clinic. "Light Therapy." MayoClinic.com (March 20, 2013). Accessed October 18, 2013. http://www.mayoclinic.com/health/light-therapy/MY00195.

[4] *Official Site / NUVIGIL*. Accessed September 16, 2013. http://www.nuvigil.com/.

Prozac Nation

[1] Centers for Disease Control and Prevention. "An Estimated 1 in 10 US Adults Report Depression." CDC.gov. (Last reviewed April 20, 2012). Accessed November 17, 2013. http://www.cdc.gov/features/dsdepression/.

[2] National Institute of Mental Health. "Depression in Children and Adolescents (Fact Sheet)." Accessed October 21, 2013. http://www.nimh.nih.gov/health/publications/depression-in-children-and-adolescents/index.shtml.

Notes

My Life Coach

[1] Robert Pagliarini. "Top 10 Professional Life Coaching Myths." CBSNews.com (December 20, 2011). Accessed March 2, 2014. http://www.cbsnews.com/news/top-10-professional-life-coaching-myths/.

[2] Berry Fowler and Associates, Inc. Fowler Academy Life Coach Training, Life Coach Certification Course (2013). Berry FIA Coaching.com. Accessed April 22, 2014. http://www.fiacoaching.com/.

Going Postal

[1] Occupational Safety & Health Administration. "Safety and Health Topics - Workplace Violence." OSHA.gov. Accessed October 21, 2013. https://www.osha.gov/SLTC/workplaceviolence/.

[2] Kyler Jae and Samantha Tata. "Father Killed in Front of Son While Answering Craigslist Ad."NBCNews.com (October 21, 2013). Accessed April 23, 2014. http://www.nbcnews.com/news/other/father-killed-front-son-while-answering-craigslist-ad.

Barbie

[1] Huffington Post. "One Third Of Young Women Would Trade Intelligence For Bigger Breasts, Survey Says." HuffingtonPost.com (March 2, 2012). Accessed May 21, 2012. http://www.huffingtonpost.com/2012/03/02/women-iq-breasts_n_1316313.html.

Reality TV—Reality? Please!

[1] Michelle Caruso. "'Extreme Makeover' Sued by Rejected Texas Mom." WiredNewYork.com (September 18, 2005). Accessed April 23, 2014. http://wirednewyork.com/forum/archive/index.php/t-7333.html.

Inquiring Minds Want to Know

[1] Wikipedia. "List of Magazines by Circulation." Wikipedia.org (Last modified April 7, 2014). Accessed April 23, 2014. http://en.wikipedia.org/wiki/List_of_magazines_by_circulation.

[2] Wikipedia. "Globe (tabloid)." Wikipedia.org (Last modified February 18, 2014). Accessed April 23, 2014. http://en.wikipedia.org/wiki/Globe_(tabloid).

[3] Wikipedia. "National Enquirer." Wikipedia.org (Last modified March 30, 2014). Accessed April 23, 2014. http://en.wikipedia.org/wiki/National_Enquirer.

The Social Disease

[1] Just Kidding!

[2] Kerry Klecic. "Internet Addiction: A Real Problem in America?" MyFoxTampaBay.com (November 5, 2013). Accessed November 26, 2013. http://www.myfoxtampabay.com/story/23877461/2013/11/05/internet-addiction-a-real-problem-in-america.

[3] Erin McClam. "Experts Increasingly Worried about 'Sextortion' of Minors Online." NBCNews.com (First published July 16, 2013). Accessed April 23, 2014. http://www.nbcnews.com/news/other/experts-increasingly-worried-about-sextortion-minors-online-f6C10645107.

The Wrongness of Political Correctness

[1] George S. Patton. "George S. Patton." WikiQuote.com (Last modified April 15, 2014). Accessed April 23, 2014. http://en.wikiquote.org/wiki/George_S._Patton.

Well Excuuuuuse Me!

[1] Rob Williams. "School in Essex Ban Triangle Shaped Flapjacks after Pupil is Hurt." Independent.co.uk (March 25, 2013). Accessed September 13, 2013. www.independent.co.uk/news/uk/home-news/school-in-essex-bans-triangle-shaped-flapjacks-after-pupil-is-hurt-8548084.html.

[2] Joe Burris. "Attorney for Student Who was Suspended for Gun-Shaped Pastry Files Appeal." BaltimoreSun.com (March 18, 2013). Accessed April 25, 2014. http://baltimoresun.com/news/maryland/bs-md-ar-pastry-gun-appeal-20130318,0,18585, print.story.

Rugged Collectivism

[1] Huffington Post. "United States Postal Service Is Losing $25 Million A Day." HuffingtonPost.com (April 17, 2013). Accessed April 25, 2014. http://www.huffingtonpost.com/2013/04/17/postal-service-losing-money-united-states_n_3104513.html.

[2] Office of Management and Budget. "Historical Tables: Table 1.1 - Summary of Receipts, Outlays, and Surpluses or Deficits(-):1789-2019." WhiteHouse.gov. Accessed April 25, 2014. http://www.whitehouse.gov/omb/budget/historicals.

[3] Anna Berkes. "Government Big Enough to Give You Everything You Want...(Quotation)." Monticello.org (Revised January 21, 2013). Accessed April 25, 2014. http://www.monticello.org/site/jefferson/government-big-enough-to-give-you-wantquotation.

[4] Wikipedia. "Aron Ralston." Wikipedia.org (Last modified June 19, 2013). Accessed April 25, 2014. http://en.wikipedia.org/wiki/Aron_Ralston.

[5] Calvin Coolidge. "Calvin Coolidge Quotes." Goodreads.com. Accessed August 28, 2013. http://www.goodreads.com/author/quotes/101882.Calvin_Coolidge.

The Persnickety Nihilist

[1] *Encarta Dictionary: English (North America), Microsoft Word, Windows 7.* Accessed September 8, 2013.

[2] Guinness World Records 2014. "Guinness out with its latest book of world records." CBSNews.com (September 12, 2013). Accessed April 25, 2014. http://www.cbsnews.com/news/guinness-out-with-its-latest-book-of-world-records/.

[3] National Day Calendar. "What National Day is Today?" NationalDayCalendar.com. Accessed September 13, 2013. http://nationaldaycalendar.com/.

[4] Mark Gerszewski. Definition of Persnickety Nihilist according to the author.

Principles?

[1] Wikipedia. "Aaron Feuerstein." Wikipedia.org (Last modified January 29, 2012). Accessed June 10, 2012. http://en.wikipedia.org/wiki/Aaron_Feuerstein.

[2] Wikipedia. "Malden Mills." Wikipedia.org (Last modified January 16, 2012). Accessed June 10, 2012. http://en.wikipedia.org/wiki/Malden_Mills.

[3] Goodreads. "Quotes About Principles." Goodreads.com. http://goodreads.com/quotes/tag/principles.

And All the Christians Say Amen

[1] Emo Philips. "Emo Philips." WikiQuote.org (Last modified April 12, 2014). Accessed April 26, 2014. http://en.wikiquote.org/wiki/Emo_Philips.

History Repeats Itself

[1] George Santayana. "George Santayana." WikiQuote.org (Last modified April 13, 2014). accessed April 26, 2014. http://en.wikiquote.org/wiki/George_Santayana.

The Owl and the Pussycat

[1] Huffington Post. "Sweden to Adopt Bestiality Ban." HuffingtonPost.com (June 13, 2013). Accessed April 26, 2014. http://huffingtonpost.com/2013/06/13/sweden-to-ban-bestiality_n_3435316.html.

[2] Huffington Post. "Erotic Zoos Prompt Germany To Reinstate Bestiality Laws." HuffingtonPost.com (November 26, 2012). Accessed April 26, 2014. http://www.huffingtonpost.com/2012/11/26/germany-bestiality-laws_n_2191677.html.

[3] Debate.org. "Bestiality Should be Legalized." Debate.org (2013). Accessed April 26, 2014. http://www.debate.org/debates/Bestiality-Should-be-Legalized/1/.

[4] Woody Allen. "I'd call him a sadistic, hippophilic necrophile, but that would be beating a dead horse. - Woody Allen." BrainyQuote.com. Accessed April 26, 2014. http://www.brainyquote.com/quotes/quotes/w/woodyallen125267.html

[5] SwissInfo.CH. "Swiss Experts Say Plants Have Rights Too." Swissinfo.ch (April 14, 2008). Accessed October 12, 2013. http://www.swissinfo.ch/eng/news_digest/Swiss_experts_say_plants_have_rights_too.html?cid=6584074.

What's So Confusing about Gender Confusion?

[1] Amanda Scherker. "Germany To Offer Third Gender Option On Birth Certificates." HuffingtonPost.com (August 17, 2013). Accessed August 17, 2013. http://www. huffingtonpost.com/2013/08/17/germany-third-gender_n_3769055.html.

[2] Perry Chiaramonte. "Controversial Therapy for Pre-Teen Transgender Patient Raises Questions." FoxNews.com (October 17, 2011). Accessed September 22, 2012. http:// www.foxnews.com/us/2011/10/17/controversial-therapy-for-young-transgender-patients-raises-questions/.

[3] Healthy Children.org. "Gender Identity and Gender Confusion In Children." HealthyChildren.org (Last updated December 30, 2011). Accessed September 22, 2012. http://www.healthychildren.org/English/ages-stages/gradeschool/pages/Gender-Identity-and-Gender-Confusion-In-Children.aspx.

[4] P. Solomon Banda and Nicholas Riccardi. "Coy Mathis Case: Colorado Civil Rights Division Rules in Favor of Transgender 6-Year-Old in Bathroom Dispute." HuffingtonPost.com (June 24, 2013). Accessed October 14, 2013. http://www.huffingtonpost.com/2013/06/24/coy-mathis_n_3488306.html.

[5] Michaela Gianotti. "California Transgender Kids Can Now Use Any Bathroom They Like." Now.MSN.com (July 5, 2013). Accessed September 29, 2013. http://now.msn.com/california-passes-transgender-rights-bill-ab-1266-1.

[6] Rebecca Klein. "Yale Adds Sex-Reassignment Surgery to Student Health Plan Coverage." HuffingtonPost.com (May 1, 2013). Accessed April 28, 2014. http://www.huffingtonpost.com/2013/05/01/yale-sex-reassignment-surgery-health-plan_n_3187564.html.

[7] Dan Reimold. "Student Fight for Gender-Neutral Dorms, Restrooms Growing on Many Campuses." College. USAToday.com (March 27, 2012). Accessed April 28, 2014. http://college.usatoday.com/2012/03/27/student-fight-for-gender-neutral-dorms-restrooms-growing-on-many-campuses/.

Where Does It All End?

[1] Confucius. "Confucius Quotes." Goodreads.com. Accessed April 28, 2014. http://www.goodreads.com/author/quotes/15321.Confucius.

Ad Nauseam: The End

[1] Albert Einstein. "Quotes by Albert Einstein." Goodreads.com. Accessed April 28, 2014. http://www.goodreads.com/quotes/724791-i-fear-the-day-technology-will-surpass-our-human-interaction.

[2] Anne Frank. "The Diary of a Young Girl," In *The Diary of a Young Girl (The Definitive Edition)* (New York: Anchor Books, 1991), 281–282.